4
Grammar through text types

PETER **DURKIN**
VIRGINIA **FERGUSON**

OXFORD
UNIVERSITY PRESS
AUSTRALIA & NEW ZEALAND

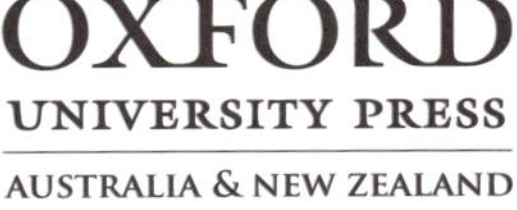

Oxford University Press is a department of the University of Oxford. It furthers the University's objective of excellence in research, scholarship, and education by publishing worldwide. Oxford is a registered trademark of Oxford University Press in the UK and in certain other countries.

Published in Australia by
Oxford University Press
Level 8, 737 Bourke Street, Docklands, Victoria 3008, Australia.

First published 2008
Reprinted 2010, 2011, 2012, 2013, 2015 (twice), 2016 (twice), 2017, 2018, 2019, 2020, 2021 (twice), 2022, 2024, 2025

ISBN 978 0 19 556039 8

Typeset Paul Ryan
Illustrated by Rob Mancini
Printed and bound in India by Manipal Technologies Limited

Acknowledgments
The author and publisher wish to thank the following copyright holders for granting permission to reproduce their material.

Getty Images p. 50 (bottom); Jupiter Unlimited pp. 26 (top & centre), 34; Newspix/Jason Simmons p. 50 (top); Photoedit p. 50 (top centre); Photolibrary p. 26 (bottom); Photolibrary/SPL p. 24; 'Moths and Moonshine' and 'Grandad lost something beginning with "T"' by James Reeves, from *Complete Poems for Children* (Heinemann), © James Reeves, reprinted with permission of the James Reeves Estate; Topfoto, p. 32; The Estate of Spike Milligan for 'On the Ning Nang Nong'.

Every effort has been made to trace the original source of copyright material contained in this book. The publisher would be pleased to hear from copyright holders to rectify any errors or omissions.

Contents

Introduction

Grammar Through Text Types uses factual and literary texts as the context for introducing basic grammar skills to primary school students:

Recount	Description	Exposition
Narrative	Explanation	Information Report
Poetry	Procedure	Transaction

The range of grammatical conventions covered meets the requirements as outlined in the state and territory standards for primary schools.

The series consists of:

- Six workbooks with 30 double-page units covering a year's work at the relevant level
- A simple answer section located at the centre of the books
- Revision units that review important grammatical conventions at word, sentence and text level.

How to use this book

The *left-hand page* of each unit focuses on a particular grammatical convention within a specific text type.

The text sample for each unit has been chosen to provide:

- examples in context of the particular grammatical convention that is the focus of that unit
- a model of a particular text type that the students can then use as a basis for their own writing.

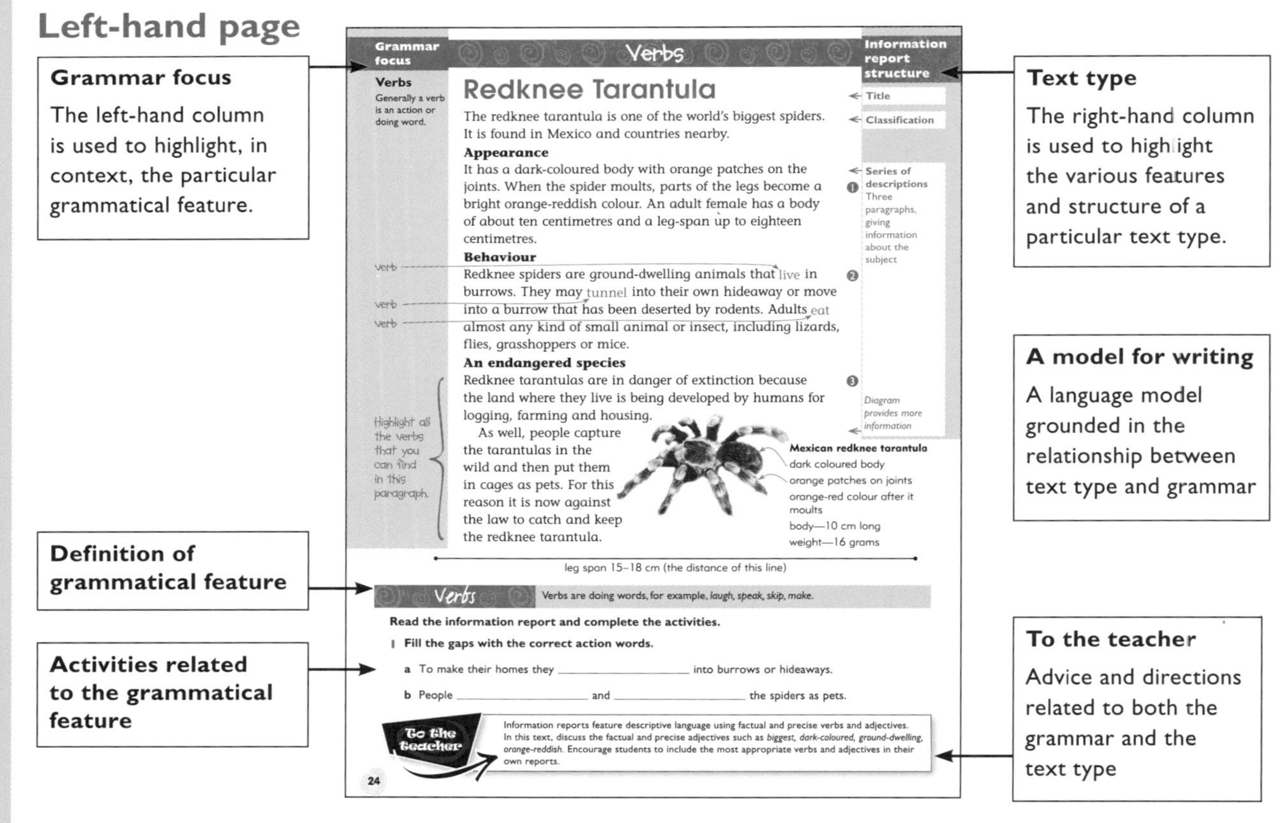

Grammar focus | Verbs | Information report structure

Verbs
Generally a verb is an action or doing word.

Redknee Tarantula ← Title

The redknee tarantula is one of the world's biggest spiders. It is found in Mexico and countries nearby. ← Classification

Appearance
It has a dark-coloured body with orange patches on the joints. When the spider moults, parts of the legs become a bright orange-reddish colour. An adult female has a body of about ten centimetres and a leg-span up to eighteen centimetres.

← Series of descriptions: Three paragraphs, giving information about the subject

Behaviour
Redknee spiders are ground-dwelling animals that live in burrows. They may tunnel into their own hideaway or move into a burrow that has been deserted by rodents. Adults eat almost any kind of small animal or insect, including lizards, flies, grasshoppers or mice.

verb / verb / verb

An endangered species
Redknee tarantulas are in danger of extinction because the land where they live is being developed by humans for logging, farming and housing.
As well, people capture the tarantulas in the wild and then put them in cages as pets. For this reason it is now against the law to catch and keep the redknee tarantula.

Highlight all the verbs that you can find in this paragraph.

Diagram provides more information

Mexican redknee tarantula
dark coloured body
orange patches on joints
orange-red colour after it moults
body—10 cm long
weight—16 grams

leg span 15–18 cm (the distance of this line)

Verbs — Verbs are doing words, for example, *laugh, speak, skip, make.*

Read the information report and complete the activities.

1 Fill the gaps with the correct action words.

a To make their homes they ______ into burrows or hideaways.

b People ______ and ______ the spiders as pets.

To the teacher: Information reports feature descriptive language using factual and precise verbs and adjectives. In this text, discuss the factual and precise adjectives such as *biggest, dark-coloured, ground-dwelling, orange-reddish.* Encourage students to include the most appropriate verbs and adjectives in their own reports.

24

Introduction

The *right-hand page* of each unit provides practice in using the grammatical skills within and beyond that specific text type. As well, this page includes an engaging *Your turn to write* section guiding the students as they apply the grammatical skills in their own writing of this particular text type.

Right-hand page

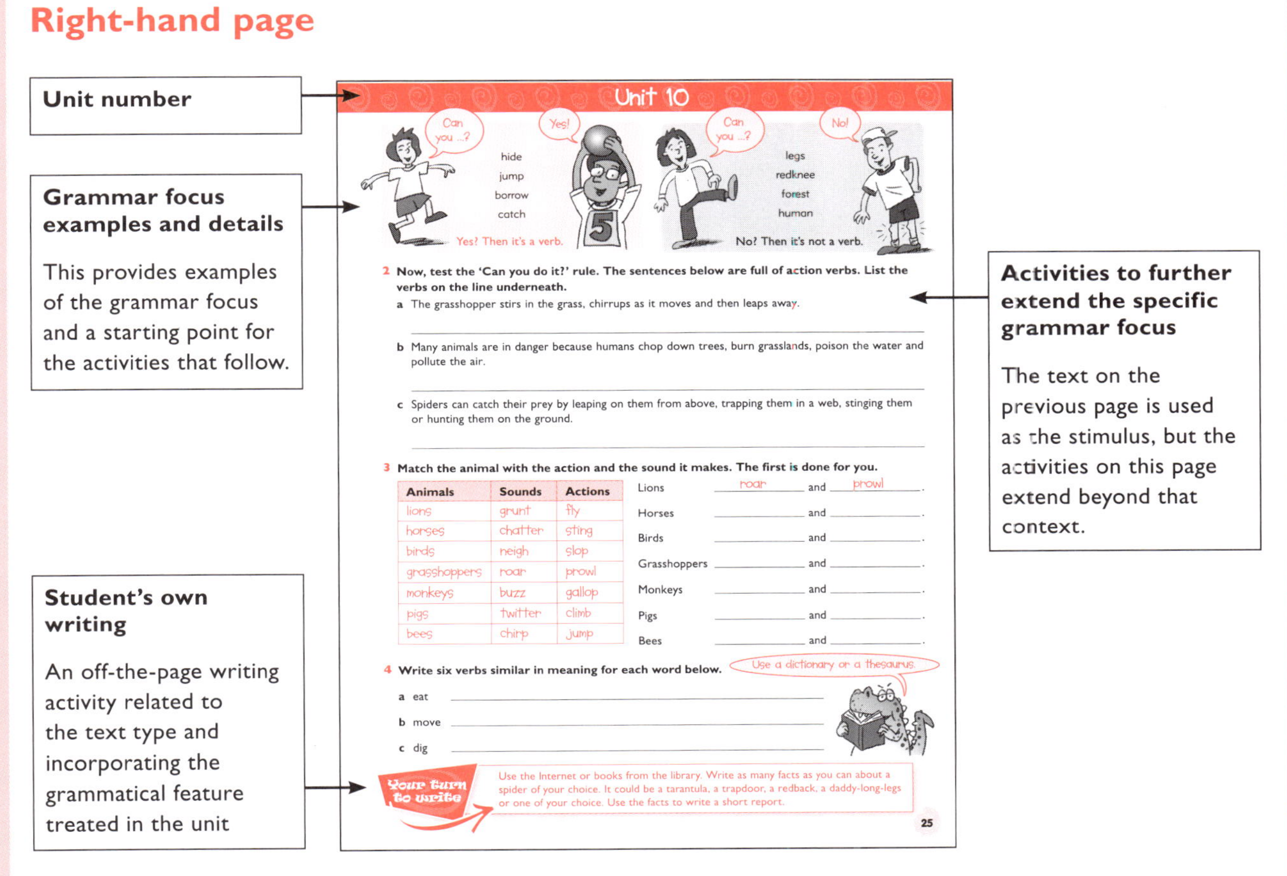

2 Now, test the 'Can you do it?' rule. The sentences below are full of action verbs. List the verbs on the line underneath.

a The grasshopper stirs in the grass, chirrups as it moves and then leaps away.

b Many animals are in danger because humans chop down trees, burn grasslands, poison the water and pollute the air.

c Spiders can catch their prey by leaping on them from above, trapping them in a web, stinging them or hunting them on the ground.

3 Match the animal with the action and the sound it makes. The first is done for you.

Animals	Sounds	Actions
lions	grunt	fly
horses	chatter	sting
birds	neigh	slop
grasshoppers	roar	prowl
monkeys	buzz	gallop
pigs	twitter	climb
bees	chirp	jump

Lions roar and prowl.
Horses ______ and ______.
Birds ______ and ______.
Grasshoppers ______ and ______.
Monkeys ______ and ______.
Pigs ______ and ______.
Bees ______ and ______.

4 Write six verbs similar in meaning for each word below. *Use a dictionary or a thesaurus.*

a eat

b move

c dig

Your turn to write Use the Internet or books from the library. Write as many facts as you can about a spider of your choice. It could be a tarantula, a trapdoor, a redback, a daddy-long-legs or one of your choice. Use the facts to write a short report.

25

Self-assessment

The assessment section provides a summary of grammatical conventions used for each text type. Grammar is assessed within the text type to enable students to evaluate their ability to use language more effectively. The assessment section looks at:

- Text Purpose
- Text Structure
- Text Forms
- Grammatical features of the relevant text type.

Students can track their progress as they proceed through the units. The assessment section can be used in collaboration with the teacher to ascertain development of, and improvement in, the acquisition of grammar skills and the capacity to apply the grammatical conventions to write in the various text types.

Nouns

Nouns are naming words.

They can be the name for:

a place

a person or animal

a feeling

a thing

The Lion and the Mouse

Title

Orientation

Once the king of the lions was sleeping deep in the forest.

Complication
Something unexpected happens

Along came a tiny mouse. "I'll creep over him," said the mouse. "He won't notice."

The king woke up and roared, "Who's spoiling my sleep?"

Sequence of events
To overcome the problem

"Only a tiny mouse," squeaked the mouse. The lion opened its huge jaws and was about to eat him up.

"Stop! If you let me go I may be able to help you one day." The lion roared with laughter. How could a tiny mouse help the king of lions? How ridiculous!

The mouse scrambled off while he could.

Resolution
The ending.

Some time later, the mouse heard a loud and angry roaring. The lion was tangled in a hunter's net, trapped and terrified. The mouse set to work. His sharp teeth nibbled for hours without stopping until at last the lion was free.

This tale teaches us a lesson.

The moral of the story is that a small friend may prove to be a great friend.

Nouns Nouns name people, places, animals, things and feelings.

Read the narrative and do the activities.

1 **Look at the title. Write the nouns for two animals.** ______________________

2 **Look at the orientation. Find nouns for these questions.**

a Where was the lion? In the ______________________

b Who was sleeping? The ______________________

3 **Look at the complication and the sequence of events. Use your highlighter. Colour in all the nouns that you can find.**

4 **Look at the resolution. Write these nouns in sentences of your own.**

a story ______________________

b friend ______________________

Narrative texts usually include many examples of common nouns, for example, *king, lion.* As well, narrative text types typically include adjectives, adverbs and direct speech. If appropriate, use the narrative above as the pretext for discussion of these grammatical features with the students.

Nouns

Everything that has a name is a noun.

Examples:

- People: girl, hunter, man, butcher
- Places: forest, mountain, beach, town
- Animals: lion, mouse, cat, mosquito
- Things: net, jaws, day, teeth
- Feelings: laughter, anger, joy, sadness

5 Choose the correct noun from the box that fits the clue.

a works in a shop, sells sausages ____________

b a place where there is sand, sea and sun ____________

c has teeth; will chomp ____________

d funny sound; made when happy ____________

6 Look at the picture of 'The lion and the mouse'. List all the nouns or names that you can see. (Don't forget the different parts of the lion, for example, *jaws*.)

____

____

____

7 Join nouns from the first net to nouns from the second net to make bigger nouns.

story, bed, key, day, butter, jaw, home, mouse

+

time, work, board, light, trap, bone, fly, room

=

Bigger nouns

jawbone

____

____

____

____

____

____

____

Look again at 'The lion and the mouse' and explain the moral of the story to a friend. Then write your own story with a moral. It could be the retelling of a famous story like 'The hare and the tortoise' or one of your own. When you write your story, remember to include in the beginning (the orientation) some nouns which name the people or animals and the place where it happens.

Grammar focus | # Nouns | **Narrative structure**

Proper nouns

Proper nouns always begin with a capital letter.

They name a particular ...

person

place

The Stone in the Road

The Mayor of Eldorado was in despair.

"This town is a disgrace," he moaned. "Rubbish is littering the streets. The people are getting lazy."

At last he worked out a plan.

That night he placed a huge stone right in the middle of Main Street. "This will test them out," he smiled.

Everyone complained, even the children and the school principal, Mrs Myrtle Brimble ...

The next day, the Mayor put up a public notice: Meeting in the Town Hall on Friday at 8 p.m.

Everyone arrived on time. "Follow me," said the Mayor. They all gathered around the stone while he heaved it to the side.

Underneath was a box: THIS IS FOR THE PERSON WHO MOVED THE STONE OFF THE ROAD.

It was filled to the brim with ancient golden coins and glittering jewels! Everyone gasped.

So, serve them right, they missed out on the treasure, but Eldorado soon became the neatest town in Australia.

Title

Orientation
Who? Where? What?

Complication

Sequence of events
To overcome the complication

Resolution
The ending

Proper nouns

Proper nouns are used for people's names or titles, and for the particular name of a place or thing. For example, *Mr Smith, Prime Minister, Bourke St., Mt. Hotham, Town Hall.*

Read the narrative and do the activities.

1 **Look at the orientation. Find a proper noun to describe the person in charge of the town.**

____

2 **Look at the sequence of events. Where was the huge stone placed?** ______________________

3 **Look at the resolution. Find the names of two places.** ______________________

4 **Use your highlighter. Colour all the proper nouns. How many are there?** ☐

Refer back to Unit 1. Discuss the distinction between a common noun, the ordinary name for something which does not begin with a capital letter, and a proper noun, which always begins with a capital letter. Also point out that the exception to this is the use of a capital letter for the beginning of a sentence.

Unit 2

Proper nouns

Proper nouns always start with a capital letter.

5 In the rock, the proper nouns have been mixed up with the common nouns. Circle the proper nouns.

6 Write a sentence using these four proper nouns: *Easter, Peter, Sunday, Dream World.*

____

____

7 Complete the certificate 'All about me'.

All about me

My full name ______________________

The town where I live ______________________

My country of birth ______________________

Three of my friends ______________________

The first names of my parents or guardians

____

The name of my school ______________________

The name of my teacher ______________________

The month of my birth ______________________

My thumb print

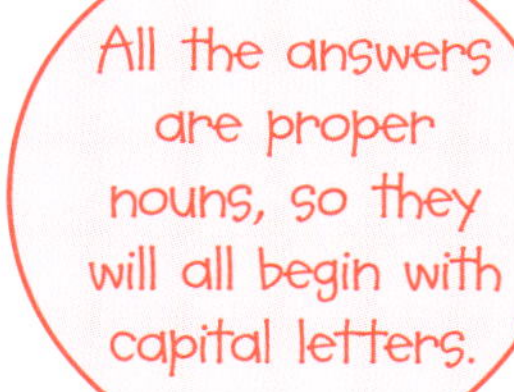

8 Write each proper noun in a sentence.

a Australia ______________________

b February ______________________

Write a story about yourself. Imagine you have done something wonderful, or heroic, or fantastic. Make sure you include in your story particular details about who was there and where and when it happened. Remember: your story must have a beginning, a middle and an end.

Grammar focus

Nouns

Narrative structure

Plural nouns ...

formed by adding 's', e.g. sausage—sausages, carrot—carrots.

formed by adding or changing letters, e.g. shelf—shelves, goose—geese.

Rotten Apples

Title

Orientation Who? What? Where

Once, on a farm, there lived a hungry old couple.

Complication

"There's nothing left to eat," cried the old woman. "No carrots, no beans, no sausages. Only a few old onions on the pantry shelves."

"We'll have to sell Daisy," said the old man.

Sequence of events First one unexpected thing happens, then the next, and the next.

Sadly, he trudged off to market. Soon he met some women leading a goat. He asked, "Would you swap your goat for my cow?"

"Certainly."

Along came two men, each carrying a goose. He asked, "Would you swap your geese for my goat?"

"Of course."

Last of all he met a man with one tooth, who was carrying a sack. They swapped. "Don't open it yet," the man said. "It's a wonderful surprise!"

The old man raced home.

"Wife, come quickly. I have a wonderful surprise!"

They ripped the sack open. It was full of rotten apples.

Conclusion Sometimes narratives have surprise endings.

His wife hugged him tight. "You clever man!" she cried. "Everyone in stories knows that rotten apples are lucky. Soon all our wishes will come true!"

And they did.

Plural nouns

Sometimes to form a plural, we add 's'. Sometimes we add 'es'. And sometimes we have to change some letters.

Read the narrative and do the activities.

1 Look at the complication.

Write five plural nouns (they all end in 's').

____

2 Look at the sequence of events, and the conclusion

a Find the plural noun for *woman*. ____________________

b Write the plurals for these words: man ____________________

goose ____________________ apple ____________________

c Write the singular for these words: teeth ____________________ wives ____________________

Talk about the structure of the narrative. In 'Rotten apples', the complication creates a series of actions, one leading quickly to another.

3 Change the words into plurals and write them in sentences. (Just add 's' to the word.)

a farm ______________________________

b cow ______________________________

c apple ______________________________

Challenge!

Change these words to the plural and write them in sentences.

pantry ______________________________

surprise ______________________________

goose ______________________________

4 Write labels for all the fruit in the bowl. If there is only one piece of fruit, write the singular name. If there is more than one, write the plural.

strawberry
orange
apple
peach
cherry
pear
watermelon
banana

5 The mystery word is part of the title of the story. Use the clues to discover what it is.

a Plural of 'farm' ....

b Singular of 'apples' ....

c Opposite of 'shuts' ....

d Opposite of 'wake' ....

e Plural of 'bean' ....

f Plural of 'sack' ....

The mystery word is

______________________________.

Your turn to write

The story 'Rotten apples' was based on 'What the old man does is always right', by Hans Christian Andersen. Rewrite a story of your own. It could be 'Rotten apples' with a different ending. What if the old woman became really angry when her husband brought home rotten apples? Or you could retell another well-known story. What if there were four little pigs, or the big bad wolf turned out to be a kind and caring beast?

Collective nouns

Collective nouns stand for a collection of things, e.g. a band of musicians.

When I Went Walking

I walked down my street and what did I see?
Just an old dog, walking after me.

I turned into Collins Street and what did I see?
A band of musicians,
And an old dog, prowling after me.

I strolled up McQuarie Street and what did I see?
A pride of lions,
A band of musicians,
And an old dog, prowling after me.

I hurried into Railway Street and what did I see?
A swarm of bees,
A pride of lions,
A band of musicians,
And an old dog, swooping after me.

I hurtled into King Street and what did I see?
A gaggle of geese,
A swarm of bees,
A pride of lions,
A band of musicians,
And an old dog, honking after me.

I dashed into Tram Street and what did I see?
A flock of birds,
A gaggle of geese,
A swarm of bees,
A pride of lions,
A band of musicians,
And an old dog, swooping after me.

I galloped into McKay Street and what did I see?
A crowd of people,
A flock of birds,
A gaggle of geese,
A swarm of bees,
A pride of lions,
A band of musicians,
And an old dog,
tumbling after me.

I limped back to my street and what did I see?
Just an old dog, walking after me.

1 **Highlight the collective nouns in 'When I went walking'.**

How many different collective nouns did you find?

To the teacher

Collective nouns include many unusual and interesting words. Make a class chart. Add to it over a number of weeks.

Collective nouns

a school of fish

a fleet of cars

a team of horses

a pair of gloves

a dozen eggs

a crew of sailors

a school of whales

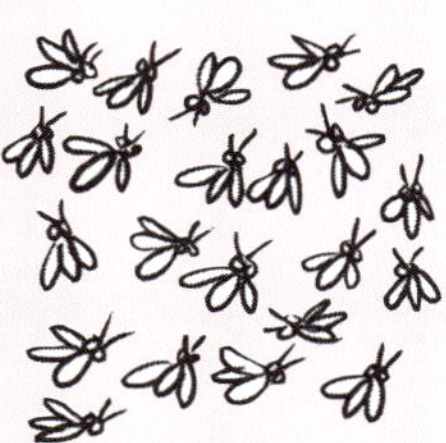

a swarm of bees

a herd of cattle

a herd of elephants

a bunch of grapes

a team of players

a forest of trees

a swarm of insects

2 A number of birds together is called a flock. Write the collective nouns for:

bees ______________ soldiers ______________

students ______________ singers ______________

ships ______________ whales ______________.

3 On my grandfather's farm I saw:

a ______________ of cattle a ______________ of chickens

a ______________ of insects a ______________ of sheep

a ______________ of kittens a ______________ of geese.

4 Write these collective nouns in sentences.

a school ______________________________

____

b pack ______________________________

____

c pair ______________________________

____

d team ______________________________

____

5 Draw lines to match the collective noun with the group.

forest	a group of pups
galaxy	a group of sailors
crew	a group of basketball players
nest	a group of mice
leap	a group of trees
litter	a group of stars
team	a group of leopards

a brood of chickens

a flock of sheep

a pride of lions

a litter of cubs

a gaggle of geese

a litter of pups

a gang of thieves

a band of musicians

an army of ants

a pack of wolves

a staff of teachers

Unusual collective nouns

a paddling of ducks

a nest of mice

a skulk of foxes

a leap of leopards

a galaxy of stars

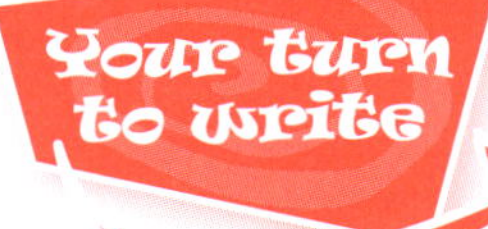

Write a word play or a rhyme based on the poem opposite. Begin with the line 'I walked down the street and what did I see?' Then use your imagination to build on the collections of different animals and things which are following you. Illustrate your rhyme with many tiny pictures.

Pronouns

Pronouns are words that take the place of nouns.

The Day My Twin Brother Sank

Title

Orientation

When I was little, we all went on a picnic in the country. I was playing by a pond with my twin brother, Cameron. Suddenly, he walked feet first into the pond. Plop!! He went straight to the bottom and then he came gurgling to the top. Then he went under and came up again. Then, as we all watched, he just went down, down, down.

The adults just stared with their mouths wide open. Then my dad shouted and my mum dashed straight into the water. She grabbed him by the hair. He was soaking and squawking.

He had clinging weeds and dripping mud oozing all over him. He looked like a black, hairy hermit, but he was all right.

Our parents and their friends took us on lots more picnics, but they never again took us close to the pond where my twin brother sank to the bottom and nearly didn't come up again.

Gemma

(Labels in margin: pronoun → I; pronoun → he; pronoun → we; pronoun → She; pronoun → they)

Sequence of events
First, he went into the water
Second, what the adults did
Third, when he was rescued

Resolution
A long concluding sentence

Pronouns

Words such as *I*, *you*, *she*, *it*, *me* and *they* are called personal pronouns.
We use personal pronouns to save repeating people's names over and over again.
For example, Cameron fell in the pond. ~~Cameron~~ He went under.

Read the recount and do the activities.

1 **Look at the orientation. Write the two personal pronouns.** ____________ ____________

2 **In this paragraph from the sequence of events, some pronouns have been left out. Write them in. (Cover the text above when you do this exercise.)**

____________ was playing by a pond with my twin brother Cameron. Suddenly, ____________ walked feet first into the pond. PLOP! ____________ went straight to the bottom and then ____________ came gurgling to the top. Then ____________ went under and came up again. Then, as ____________ all watched, ____________ just went down, down, down.

Ask the students to circle all the pronouns in the text. Then ask them to identify the nouns (names) which each pronoun replaced.

Note that in recounts, action verbs, as well as pronouns, predominate. If appropriate, focus on the action verbs above, for example, *walked*, *gurgling*, *watched*.

Demonstrate to the students that the structure of recounts is very similar to that of narratives.

3 **Below is a list of pronouns.**

I	we	me	us	you	he	she
they	him	her	them	theirs	his	yourself
ourselves	themselves	mine	hers	myself	himself	

Write the pronouns in their correct boxes.

Just about me	Male pronouns	Female pronouns	Groups
me	him	she	themselves, us

4 **Rewrite each sentence, using *he, she, it* or *they* to take the place of the nouns or noun groups in bold. The first one is done for you.**

a **Cameron** couldn't swim. He couldn't swim.

b **The adults** just stared. ____________

c **The water** was dark and murky. ____________

d **My mum** dashed into the water. ____________

e **My dad** just shouted. ____________

f **Gemma** is Cameron's twin sister. ____________

g **Our parents** took us on lots of picnics. ____________

5 **Write the pair of words in one sentence.**

Mum / she ____________

6 **The extract below tells us more about the twins. Circle all the pronouns.**

The writer of the recount is Gemma. The name of her twin brother is Cameron. He is the one who fell in the water. The parents of the twins are Hugh and Lorna. This recount is true. Cameron really did fall in the pond and all the rest of us were so shocked that we did not jump to his rescue straight away. Cameron and Gemma are now twenty-three. She lives in Melbourne and he lives on the Gold Coast.

How many pronouns did you find? ☐

Write a recount about a time when something surprising, shocking or sensational happened to you or your family. You will need to use lots of pronouns in your recount. When you have finished, count how many pronouns you used.

Pronouns

Personal pronouns

Personal pronouns take the place of nouns that are doing the action.

personal pronouns
i, you, he, she, it, we, they, me, him, her, us, them

Possessive pronouns

Possessive pronouns take the place of nouns that are owned by someone or something. e.g. as good as *mine*

possessive pronouns
mine, yours, his, hers, its, ours, theirs

Jim's Diary

Wednesday 4 March
Dear Diary,
Mum dropped a bombshell today. She made an appointment for me to go to the dentist in ten days' time. "If you look after your teeth, they'll be just as good as mine," she said.

← Orientation

Thursday 5 March
Dear Diary,
Can't think of anything else but dentists and I don't even have a toothache!

← Sequence of events

Wednesday 11 March
Dear Diary,
Three days to go. It's amazing how some things work on your mind. I've even given up lollies and biscuits.

Friday 13 March
Dear Diary,
Unlucky Friday 13. One day till D-Day. All I can think of is that buzzing drill and that pointy, prongy thing.

Saturday 14 March
Dear Diary,
D-Day. Dentist day !!!! Sitting in that waiting room was bad. Then it was my time to go in. The dentist said "Open wide!" He prodded and poked and talked and prodded and talked some more. He wanted me to talk. "It's all right for you," I thought. "Your mouth is not full of stuff and stuck open like mine!" Suddenly he stopped. "That's all for you, my boy. Your teeth are perfect. Not a single thing to do. I wish everybody looked after their teeth like you look after yours."

Sunday 15 March
Dear Diary,
One day after D-Day. Happiness!
Freedom! Bliss!

← Personal or evaluative comments

Pronouns

Remember, pronouns take the place of nouns.

Read the recount and do the activities.

1 **Look again at Jim's diary, and highlight all the pronouns that you can find.**

2 **Write four pronouns you have highlighted for the diary entry Saturday 14 March.**

____________ ____________ ____________ ____________

Discuss possessive pronouns (ownership) and personal pronouns. The personal pronouns *she, me, you, I* and *he* are in the diary. Ask the students to find and circle these.
Discuss diaries and journals as forms of recount. Why are they classified as recounts?

Personal pronouns

Personal pronouns take the place of nouns that are doing the action.

I	we	her	he
him	she	they	us
it	me	them	you

3 Choose the best personal pronouns to fill the gaps.

a ____________ fixed the bike so it was as good as new.

b Yesterday ____________ woke up really early.

c After ____________ went shopping, ____________ went to the beach.

d ____________ likes to talk a lot.

e ____________ brushed his teeth really well.

f ____________ thought the pencil was mine, but Leila said it was hers.

Possessive pronouns

Possessive pronouns show ownership.

4 Write these possessive pronouns in sentences.

a ours ______________________________

b theirs ______________________________

c yours ______________________________

d mine ______________________________

e hers ______________________________

5 Choose the best possessive pronouns to fill the gaps.

mine	hers	his	its	ours	theirs

a The pencils on the desk are ____________.

b Our class is smaller than ____________.

c Is that sunhat ____________?

d Your hair is blacker than ____________.

e ____________ is the one on the top shelf.

f These shorts are ____________.

Your turn to write

Write a recount about a time when you visited the dentist. See if you can include these six pronouns in your recount: *I, mine, he, his, hers, me.*

Grammar focus

Adjectives

Recount structure

Adjectives

An adjective is a describing word.

No School Today

Title

Orientation: When? Who? What? Where?

It was a beautiful, sunny Thursday morning with a spiky frost on the ground. Pramit, my best friend, and I were walking to school when someone came waving and shouting. "No school today. The teacher is sick." (We went to a one-teacher school in the country and when the teacher was away, the school closed down.)

Sequence of events

Hooray! We were free! We decided to go lizard hunting, one of our best games. We went down to the creek in the back (adjective) paddock, where the sun warmed the rocks. Often, under a rock, there was a lizard which we captured, put in a glass (adjective) container and let go later. We had caught a few when I saw a scaly (adjective) tail sticking out from under a rock. I grabbed it. YOW!! It was a snake. I let it go and ran.

Concluding comment

That was the last of lizard hunting for us!

Adjectives tell us something about the noun or pronoun. They may tell how much, how many, what kind or what position.

Read the recount and do the activities.

1 Read the orientation. Find three adjectives which describe what kind of morning it was.

____

2 Read the sequence of events. Which adjectives tell us about these nouns?

a games ______________ **b** paddock ______________

c container ______________ **d** tail ______________

3 Find the adjective which describes frost. List adjectives of your own to describe frost.

____

4 Use these adjectives in sentences.

a scaly ______________________________

b spiky ______________________________

c best ______________________________

In simple personal recounts such as this one, language features include action verbs (*caught*, *grabbed*) and temporal connectives (*when*, *later*). Recounts are typically written in the past tense. Most recounts (including this one) contain adjectives and groups of words to describe nouns. Ask the students to circle all the nouns they can find. Then highlight in red any adjectives which describe those nouns. NB. Advise students that they should not collect reptiles in the wild.

Adjectives

Adjectives describe people, places and things. They also tell us about:

- colour: The pupil has a *black* eye.
- shape: The teacher has *square* glasses.
- how many: You are *two* minutes late.
- size: The teacher has *big* teeth and *long* legs.

5 **Fill the blanks in the cartoon with the missing adjectives.**

6 **Circle the adjectives in the sentences.**

a The teacher has square glasses.

b He has a pointy nose.

c He is wearing long black trousers.

d The pupil has spiky hair and a sniffly nose.

7 **Put each adjective and noun into a sentence.**

a spiky / hair ______

b loud / voice ______

c bad / accident ______

8 **Circle the adjectives which describe the nouns in orange.**

Going to a one-teacher school was great fun. In my little school there were only twelve children. There were two preps and three children in my Grade 4. The oldest person in the school was in Grade 6. He was the only one in that grade. There was just one big room and one wide blackboard. The teacher put the work for the whole school on that blackboard. During play times and lunch times we were allowed to play in the cow paddock and climb the tallest trees. Of course, the best time of all was when the teacher was away. Then the school was closed and we had a holiday.

Find three different adjectives to describe 'school' in question 8.

Your turn to write

Write a recount about something that happened to you at school, or when you were going to or from school. Make sure your recount contains descriptions including colour, shape, how many and how much, and adjectives to describe the things that have happened.

Adjectives

Adjectives are used to add extra information about nouns.

Bird Concert

Title

The bird concert happens every spring time way up high in the treetops in the mountains. The birds come for the wild bird seed that we leave in a tray on a branch of a big black wattle tree. This is what happens.

Introduction

Adjectives describe the noun.

First come the rainbow lorikeets with a ping and a clattery chatter. They line up all in a row and take it in turns to eat the bird seed.

Next comes the currawong. His sad song tells of rain and distant storms. He is a huge, black bird, with white patches and a wild, staring amber eye. Currawongs eat everything—seeds, plants and tiny birds—so the lorikeets fly away. When the currawong leaves, the lorikeets return.

Description
A series of details about the bird concert

The adjective tiny tells us more about the noun birds.

Then in swoops the magpie. His warbling and chortling is a waterfall of sound. He frightens the lorikeets, but not for long. They sneak back and peck at the seed when the magpie is not looking.

Last comes the giant white cockatoo with a yellow beak and curling, clasping claws. He is the loudspeaker of the birds whose throaty, rasping crackle-call tells everybody to "look-out" because it is seed-cracking time. When the cocky flies off the lorikeets come back and chatter and crunch and scramble on the branch.

Then suddenly they are all gone and just for a moment you can hear the silence in the mountaintops.

Concluding statement

Adjectives

We use adjectives to tell us more about people, places, animals and things.

Read the description and do the activities.

1 Fill the spaces with adjectives from the description.

a The currawong is a ______________ ______________ bird, with ______________ patches and a ______________ ______________ ______________ eye.

b The white cockatoo has a ______________ beak and ______________ ______________ claws.

2 Use the word 'amber' in a sentence. (Think of traffic lights.)

____

The description above is about a particular place in the Dandenong Ranges. The description combines the presentation of everyday facts with literary description. Ask the students to highlight all the adjectives in the description. Then, as a class, look at the poetic qualities in the writing and the way that the writer uses literary techniques (metaphor, onomatopoeia) to recreate the sounds and the atmosphere of the forest.

Adjectives

Always choose the best adjective to describe the noun.

CHALLENGE
'Amber' is a colour in the currawong's eyes. What shades of colour can you think of to describe the rainforest?

3 Circle the best adjective for each noun.

- **a** lion — gentle, ragged, fierce, lonely, tired
- **b** spider — little, red, poisonous, friendly, tearful
- **c** greyhound — hungry, floppy, speedy, small, grumpy
- **d** carrot — crunchy, round, smelly, flimsy, secretive

4 Fill the boxes with adjectives. Choose words similar in meaning to the word in each box. Use your thesaurus to help.

noisy	large	wild

The opposite of 'noisy' is ______________.

The opposite of 'large' is ______________.

The opposite of 'wild' is ______________.

5 In the spaces, use adjectives to describe what these birds look like and the sounds they make. (The first one is done for you.)

a The magpie The magpie is a noisy bird with black and white feathers. It has a sharp beak. The magpie makes a sweet, musical, warbling sound.

b The kookaburra ______________________________

c The budgerigar ______________________________

d The cockatoo ______________________________

Choose your favourite bird. Find out all you can about it. Write a description of it. Use adjectives to describe what it looks like and the sound it makes.

Sentences
A sentence is a group of words that make sense on their own.

Roald Dahl—A Biography

← Title

← Orientation

Roald Dahl was born on 13 September 1916. He married the actress Patricia Neal in 1953. They had three children and later separated.

← Sequence of events
Early life

Roald Dahl said he had "a very ordinary life", but that was not true at all. He flew planes in World War II. He survived a crash, worked as a kind of spy and later became a Wing Commander. He disliked school. The only things he was good at were sport and passing exams. One report said, "I have never met a boy who so often writes the exact opposite of what he means." Another stated, "He is a persistent muddler … he reminds me of a camel."

A sentence begins with a capital letter.

It ends with a full stop.

Likes and dislikes

He loved wine, chocolate, painting, music and gardening. He would have loved to have been a doctor. He said that "pop singers are horrible" and he refused to eat tripe.

← Conclusion
Some of his books

Some of his well-known books include:

- *James and the Giant Peach*
- *Charlie and the Chocolate Factory*
- *The BFG*
- *The Twits*
- *George's Marvellous Medicine.*

By Peter and Virginia

Sentences

A sentence is a complete thought. It always makes sense. It always ends with a punctuation mark. This could be a full stop (.), a question mark (?) or an exclamation mark (!).

Read the biography and do the activities.

1 Circle the sentences. (Remember a sentence must make sense.)

a The only things
b He was good at sport.
c On 13 September 1916
d Roald Dahl wrote many books.
e Never met a boy who
f They had three children.

2 Complete the sentences.

a My favourite author is ______________________________

b My favourite book is ______________________________

A simple sentence has just one clause that makes sense on its own. Focus at this level on simple sentences. Examine with the students the nature of a clause (a group of words that expresses a complete thought).

Talk about the biography of Roald Dahl. A biography is a recount of a person's life, written by another person.

3 Write sentences to answer the questions. (The first one is done for you.)

a When was Roald Dahl born?

Roald Dahl was born in 1916.

b What was his wife's occupation?

______

c How many children did they have?

______

d What were some things that Roald Dahl loved?

______

e What were three things that he disliked?

______

f Roald Dahl reminded one of his teachers of an animal. What was it?

______

4 Write a sentence from the biography which contains:

a less than four words ______

b three or more commas ______

c quotation marks. ______

5 Make complete sentences by joining the subject, verb and object.

Subject	Verb	Object
Cats	is	three children.
The footballer	had	an author.
Roald Dahl	kicked	the ladder.
The fireman	like	the hare.
Monkeys	is	trees.
Our teacher	climbed	milk.
The tortoise	climb	kind.
Roald and Patricia	beat	the ball.

Choose somebody that you admire a lot. Use the model opposite to write a short biography of that person. Remember to include the date of birth, some interesting facts and some reasons why the person is special.

Verbs
Generally a verb is an action or doing word.

Redknee Tarantula

Title

The redknee tarantula is one of the world's biggest spiders. It is found in Mexico and countries nearby.

Classification

Appearance

It has a dark-coloured body with orange patches on the joints. When the spider moults, parts of the legs become a bright orange-reddish colour. An adult female has a body of about ten centimetres and a leg-span up to eighteen centimetres.

Series of descriptions
Three paragraphs, giving information about the subject

1

Behaviour

Redknee spiders are ground-dwelling animals that live in burrows. They may tunnel into their own hideaway or move into a burrow that has been deserted by rodents. Adults eat almost any kind of small animal or insect, including lizards, flies, grasshoppers or mice.

2

verb (live)
verb (tunnel)
verb (eat)

An endangered species

Redknee tarantulas are in danger of extinction because the land where they live is being developed by humans for logging, farming and housing.

As well, people capture the tarantulas in the wild and then put them in cages as pets. For this reason it is now against the law to catch and keep the redknee tarantula.

3

Highlight all the verbs that you can find in this paragraph.

Diagram provides more information

Mexican redknee tarantula
dark coloured body
orange patches on joints
orange-red colour after it moults
body—10 cm long
weight—16 grams

leg span 15–18 cm (the distance of this line)

Verbs Verbs are doing words, for example, *laugh, speak, skip, make.*

Read the information report and complete the activities.

1 Fill the gaps with the correct action words.

a To make their homes they ____________ into burrows or hideaways.

b People ____________ and ____________ the spiders as pets.

Information reports feature descriptive language using factual and precise verbs and adjectives. In this text, discuss the factual and precise adjectives such as *biggest, dark-coloured, ground-dwelling, orange-reddish.* Encourage students to include the most appropriate verbs and adjectives in their own reports.

2 Now, test the 'Can you do it?' rule. The sentences below are full of action verbs. List the verbs on the line underneath.

a The grasshopper stirs in the grass, chirrups as it moves and then leaps away.

____

b Many animals are in danger because humans chop down trees, burn grasslands, poison the water and pollute the air.

____

c Spiders can catch their prey by leaping on them from above, trapping them in a web, stinging them or hunting them on the ground.

____

3 Match the animal with the action and the sound it makes. The first is done for you.

Animals	Sounds	Actions
lions	grunt	fly
horses	chatter	sting
birds	neigh	slop
grasshoppers	roar	prowl
monkeys	buzz	gallop
pigs	twitter	climb
bees	chirp	jump

Lions roar and prowl.

Horses ________ and ________.

Birds ________ and ________.

Grasshoppers ________ and ________.

Monkeys ________ and ________.

Pigs ________ and ________.

Bees ________ and ________.

4 Write six verbs similar in meaning for each word below.

Use a dictionary or a thesaurus.

a eat ____________________________

b move ____________________________

c dig ____________________________

Your turn to write

Use the Internet or books from the library. Write as many facts as you can about a spider of your choice. It could be a tarantula, a trapdoor, a redback, a daddy-long-legs or one of your choice. Use the facts to write a short report.

Verbs

Verbs tell about the action of a sentence.

Built for Speed

Title

The fastest creatures on Earth are built to move quickly. They use their speed to hunt their prey. The cheetah is the fastest creature on land, the peregrine falcon the quickest through the air and the sail fish the fastest marine creature.

General statement or classification

Series of descriptions and diagrams

The focus in the description is on how the creatures can catch their prey.

Cheetahs are built for speed. They rely on quick bursts to catch their prey. They often knock their prey to the ground before stopping them with a deadly bite. Cheetahs must eat quickly to stop other animals from stealing their prey.

Cheetah

Top speed: 112 kph

Peregrine falcons sit in tall dead trees or soar high above the ground looking for animals to eat. When they spot their prey they swoop towards the ground, diving at speeds of more than 320 kilometres per hour. Usually they stun their prey and then carry it to a sheltered place where they tear it to pieces and swallow it.

verb

verb

verb

Every sentence has at least one verb.

Peregrine falcon

Top speed: 321 kph

Sail fish work together to catch their favourite food such as tuna or mackerel. First they pursue their prey at half speed, then they chase the school at full speed. They hit the prey with their bills to stun them and then eat the fish, usually head first.

Use a highlighter to colour all the verbs in this paragraph.

Sail fish

Top speed: 110 kph

The fastest humans run at about 37 kilometres per hour, so it just goes to show how much faster some birds, fish and animals can move.

Summarising comment

Read the report and do the activities.

1 **How do the animals catch their prey? Complete the sentences and underline the verbs you have used.**

a Cheetahs catch their prey by ____________________

b Peregrine falcons catch their prey by ____________________

A grammatical feature of information reports is the use of timeless present-tense verbs. Use this text to introduce tense. First, identify the verbs and then discuss tense, for example, *move* (present), *moved* (past) and *will move* (future).

2 Read the information report again, and then do the verb search.

a Look at the general statement and find two action verbs.

____

b Read the paragraph on the cheetah to find verbs similar in meaning to:

capture ________ hit ________ thieving ________ chew ________.

c There are at least ten action verbs in the paragraph on the peregrine falcon. List them.

____

3 Choose the best verb from the box to complete each sentence.

soar	hunt	screech	croak	laugh
caw	pounce	sing	tumble	slide

a Kookaburras ________.

b Falcons ________.

c Cockatoos ________.

d Crows ________.

e Whales ________.

f Clowns ________.

g Snails ________.

h Tigers ________.

i Wolves ________.

j Bullfrogs ________.

4 The peregrine falcon is high up in the tall dead tree. Its tiny prey is way below near a burrow in the grasslands.
Fill the spaces with action verbs to describe what the falcon can do and what its prey could do.

hide

soar

Your turn to write

Write an information report about a topic that you are studying in class. Find out many facts before you begin. Use colourful illustrations to help make your report interesting and informative. Remember to include action verbs in your sentences.

Verbs
Verbs are action words which sometimes take the form of commands, e.g. *Put …*, *Insert …*, *Choose ….*

How to Check Your Heartbeat

← Title

Goal ← Goals

To discover how many times your heart beats in a minute:
- first, when you are resting
- second, after you have exercised.

What you need ← Materials
- rubber tubing (approximately 90 cm)
- two funnels (cut the top sections off plastic soft drink bottles)
- masking tape
- stopwatch

What to do ← Sequence of steps

1 Put one of the funnels into one end of the rubber tubing.
2 Attach it with masking tape.
3 Insert the other funnel into the other end of the rubber tubing and attach it with masking tape.
4 Choose a good place to rest.

5 While you sit quietly, place one funnel over your heart.
6 Put the other funnel over your ear.
7 Carefully count the number of heartbeats that you hear in 30 seconds. Double this and write down the result.
8 Some time later, run around the school oval or basketball court. Then count the number of heartbeats in 30 seconds.

Action words (commands)

Did it work? ← (Evaluation)

Did your heartbeat increase after exercise? By how much did it increase? If you have counted correctly and your heartbeat has increased, then your experiment has worked.

Commands

Commands are sentences that begin with action verbs. They usually tell someone to do something.

Read the procedure and then do the activities.

1 **Highlight all the verbs you can find in the 'What to do' section.**

2 **Circle the verbs in the 'What to do' section which are at the beginning of the sentence.**

How many are there? ______

The instructions in a procedure often begin with a command such as *Choose, Put, Attach*. The sentences are usually short and sometimes include information on how the action should be done, for example, "Carefully count the number of heartbeats …". The commands in procedures are verbs. The 'how' words are adverbs.

3 **Write instructions for crossing the road. Begin each new sentence with an action verb.**

Crossing the road safely—Instructions

1 ______

2 ______

3 ______

4 ______

5 ______

4 **What are the people saying? Write in the speech bubbles. Don't forget the action verb.**

STOP

5 **Write these action words in sentences of your own: *squeeze, rub, glue, shake*.**

______

______

______

______

Test the heart rates of the people in your class. Work out how you will test the resting rate and the active rate. Record the rates of each person. Present the results as a bar graph that shows the active and resting rate of each person.

Adverbs

Adverbs tell us more about verbs.

Find the Lost Treasure

← Goal

Materials you will need

A map of Skull Island

The adverb carefully tells us more about the verb climb.

verb

adverb

Instructions for finding the lost treasure

1 Begin at Point Misery. Walk slowly because there are snakes in the grasslands.
2 Climb carefully over the Grim Peaks. Continue in a north-west direction.
3 Travel north towards Desolation Cave. (Move carefully around the Sinking Sand.)
4 Pick up the shovel from the cave. Head west.
5 Travel quickly to Crocodile Creek. You will arrive easily within an hour.
6 Walk slowly and watchfully around Crocodile Creek.
7 Keep travelling towards the rock which is clearly marked with the skull and crossbones.
8 Dig directly under the crossbones.

* The treasure is two metres down.

Read the instructions and complete the activities.

1 **Using a pen, trace the journey from Point Misery to the treasure.**

2 **Adverbs tell us more about verbs. Use highlighters to mark verbs and circle the adverbs. Remember: adverbs often end in 'ly', for example, *quickly, slowly*.**

Unit 13

Adverbs

Adverbs tell us more about an action. For example, *John walked quickly*.

3 Underline the adverbs in the sentences and write the verb that it describes. (In some sentences there is more than one adverb.)

This one is done for you.

a Watch carefully for snakes in the grasslands. ____watch____

b You must climb slowly to save your energy. ______________

c When you get near quicksand, walk slowly and gently. ______________

d The creek is full of crocodiles which attack ferociously and angrily. ______________

e Beware of the cunningly hidden trap door at the skull and crossbones. ______________

f When you find the treasure, go quickly from the island. ______________

4 Change these adjectives to adverbs.

a clear ______________ b easy ______________ c slow ______________

d careful ______________ e quick ______________ f brave ______________

5 Choose two of the adverbs above to write your own sentence.

____

____

6 Choose the most suitable word from the box to complete each sentence.

triumphantly	dangerously	frantically	silently	gently	slowly	angrily

a "That's my map," snarled the pirate ______________.

b The boys walked ______________ close to the quicksand.

c The waves lapped ______________ onto the shores of Shipwreck Bay.

d The pirate ran ______________ from the snapping crocodile.

e The shark slid ______________ through the water.

f The exhausted man ______________ climbed the Grim Peaks.

g "We've found the treasure!" they shouted ______________.

Your turn to write

Write a set of instructions on 'How I get to school'. Draw a map with compass points and include illustrations of places and things along the way. Remember to use action verbs and adverbs which tell more about those verbs. Ask a friend to read your instructions and decide how good they are.

Adverbs

Adverbs tell how, when and where about the verb.

How to Make Invisible Ink

← Title

Goal

To make invisible ink that your friend can read easily but that will be invisible to others ← Goal

Materials

← Materials

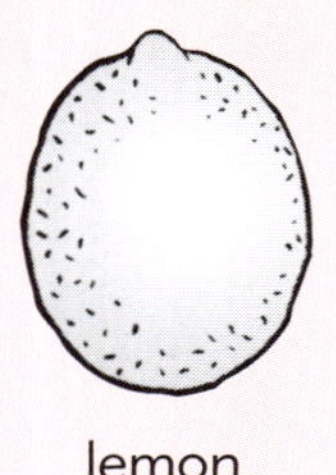
lemon

old-fashioned pen with steel nib, or a fountain pen

paper

reading light

What to do

← Sequence of steps

Adverb telling 'how' about the verb →

1 Before beginning, carefully cut a ripe lemon in two. Squeeze the juice of the lemon into a juicer.

2 Use a funnel to slowly pour the liquid into a small container.

Adverb telling 'when' about the verb →

3 Next, select an old-fashioned pen with a steel nib, or a fountain pen.

4 Dip the pen into the liquid and write down your message neatly on a blank sheet of paper. Make sure you write legibly.

5 Place it nearby on a desk or table to dry. When your writing dries, it should be invisible.

6 Now send the message to your friend.

Adverb telling 'where' about the verb →

7 Explain that for the message to become visible, it must be held near a reading light. It should be held near the light, but not too close. The heat from the light will make the lemon-juice writing visible.

Evaluation

Could your friend read the message easily? If the answer was "yes", then your experiment was successful. If the answer was "no", try again or experiment with other liquids such as onions, vinegar, milk or salt mixed with water. ← Evaluation

Read the procedure and do the activities.

1 Look at the goal. Write an adverb ending in 'ly'. ____________________

2 Look at the 'What to do' instructions. Find four adverbs telling 'how' about the verb. They all end in 'ly'.

____

To the teacher

If a steel nib is too difficult to find, a fountain pen is just as effective (with no ink, of course). Discuss 'how', 'when' and 'where' adverbs. In a class discussion, highlight the 'where' and 'when' adverbs.

Adverbs

Adverbs can tell us how, when and where about the verb. For example:

Firmly squeeze the lemon. (how)
Next, select an old-fashioned pen. (when)
Leave your writing *nearby*. (where)

3 Write each adverb in the correct box.

then	soon	near	here	there	quickly	firmly
outside	when	slowly	afterwards	carefully	legibly	next
by	up	yesterday	down	gently	inside	

'how' adverbs	'when' adverbs	'where' adverbs

4 Change these adjectives into adverbs by adding 'ly'. Be careful. Some are tricky!

a kind kindly　　**b** easy ______　　**c** clever ______

d noisy ______　　**e** truthful ______　　**f** simple ______

g firm ______　　**h** clumsy ______　　**i** silent ______

5 Write these adverbs in sentences.

a happily ______

______

b when ______

______

c inside ______

______

6 Circle the adverbs in the word search.

t	h	e	r	e	s	n	c
w	w	r	a	o	o	a	l
n	b	y	r	c	o	s	e
e	e	e	f	e	n	l	a
a	f	a	t	o	a	o	r
r	o	s	i	w	f	w	l
b	r	i	g	h	t	l	y
y	e	l	e	e	e	y	e
r	w	y	l	n	r	o	t

Write a message in invisible ink to a friend. The message must be so funny, or secretive, or personal, that only your friend can know about it.

Sentences (Revision)

Headline

Introduction paragraph
Tell who, what, when, where.

Young Girl Fights Crocodile

Yesterday a young girl became a heroine. She saved a man from the jaws of a crocodile. The incident happened at about midday, Northern Territory time. The girl, Peta-Lynn Martin (13), jumped into the murky waters of a crocodile-infested river to help her friend, Hilton Graham (23).

At the time of the attack, Peta-Lyn and her friend were looking for wild pigs. Their boat got stuck in the mud. Hilton jumped overboard in an attempt to free it. While he was in the water the crocodile attacked. It launched itself into the air and grabbed Hilton by the left arm. Peta-Lyn instantly jumped to the rescue. She grabbed Hilton's free arm.

The crocodile was pulling Hilton towards deeper water so that it could get a better grip on him. "I used all my strength to keep him in shallower water," said Peta-Lyn. Suddenly the croc let go and Peta-Lyn pulled Hilton towards the bank. But the crocodile came back. "This time it got his right leg and started spinning him around, but I still had a firm grip on his right arm." Again the croc let go. This gave Peta-Lyn time to drag the wounded man to the river bank.

Somehow Peta-Lyn got the big man into his car and then drove him back home. From there, they contacted Darwin for help.

"He's a lucky young man," said the ambulance officer, who attended Hilton. "He has lost a lot of blood, but he will be fine after a few days in hospital."

Sentences

Remember: a sentence is a group of words which make sense. A sentence begins with a capital letter and ends with a full stop.

Read the newspaper report and do the activities.

1 Write the answers in complete sentences.

a Who is the article about? The article is about ______________________

____

b What is it about? ______________________

____

c Where did it happen? ______________________

____

d When did it happen? ______________________

____

Discuss the newspaper article. Newspaper articles are a form of recount. Note the use of past-tense verbs, the orientation with the questions on who, what, when, where; the use of reported speech and the frequent use of pronouns. When the students answer the who, what, when, where questions, they must answer in complete sentences which contain a subject and a verb and they must make sense.

Answer pages

Unit 1

1 lion, mouse. **2 a)** forest. **b)** lion. **3** mouse, king, sleep, jaws, day, laughter, king, lions. **4** Teacher. **5 a)** butcher. **b)** beach. **c)** lion. **d)** laughter. **6** clouds, sun, birds, trees, mouse, monkey, lion, net, mane, paws, eyes, nose, teeth, tail, claws. **7** storytime, bedroom, keyboard, daylight, butterfly, homework, mousetrap.

Unit 2

1 Mayor. **2** Main Street. **3** Eldorado, Australia. **4** 8. **5** Australia, Friday, Town Hall, Mrs Brimble, Easter, Main Street, Mayor, Eldorado. **6–8** Teacher.

Unit 3

1 carrots, sausages, beans, onions, shelves. **2 a)** woman. **b)** men, geese, apples. **c)** tooth, wife. **3 a)** farms. **b)** cows. **c)** apples. **Challenge** pantries, surprises, geese. **4** strawberries, apple, cherries, watermelon, orange, peach, pears, bananas. **5** farms, apple, opens, sleep, beans, sacks. **Mystery word:** apples.

Unit 4

1 6 (band, pride, swarm, gaggle, flock, crowd). **2** bees – swarm, soldiers – army, students – class, singers – choir, ships – fleet, whales – school. **3** a herd of cattle, a brood of chickens, a swarm of insects, a flock of sheep, a team of horses, a gaggle of geese. **4** Teacher. **5** a group of pups – litter, a group of sailors – crew, a group of basketball players – team, a group of mice – nest, a group of trees – forest, a group of stars – galaxy, a group of leopards – leap.

Unit 5

1 I, we. **2** I, he, He, he, he, we, he. **3 Just about me** I, mine, myself. **Male pronouns** he, his, himself. **Female pronouns** her, hers. **Groups** us, you, we, they, them, theirs, ourselves, themselves. **4 b)** They just stared. **c)** It was dark and murky. **d)** She dashed into the water. **e)** He just shouted. **f)** She is his twin sister. **g)** They took us on lots of picnics. **5** Teacher. **6** her, He, us, we, his, She, he – 7.

Unit 6

1 she, me, you, they, mine, I, It, I, I, it, He, He. me, It, you, mine, he, you, I, you, yours. **2** it, he, me, you, I, mine, yours. **3** Teacher. **4** Teacher. **5** Teacher.

Unit 7

1 beautiful, sunny, Thursday. **2 a)** best. **b)** back. **c)** glass. **d)** scaly. **3** spiky, icy, chilly, nippy, biting. **4** Teacher. **5** two, square, big, black, long. **6 a)** square. **b)** pointy. **c)** long, black. **d)** spiky, sniffly. **7** Teacher. **8** one-teacher, little, twelve, oldest, one big, one wide, whole, tallest, best.

Unit 8

1 a) huge, black, white, wild, staring, amber. **b)** yellow, curling, clasping. **2** Teacher. **3 a)** fierce. **b)** poisonous. **c)** speedy. **d)** crunchy. **Challenge** Teacher. **4 noisy –** lively, rowdy, blaring, shrill, thundering, loud, booming, deafening. **large –** big, enormous, giant, gigantic, great, huge, immense, outsize, oversized, vast, massive. **wild –** free, ferocious, savage, untamed, rough, excited, reckless, rowdy, crazy, rough. **Opposites:** noisy – quiet, large – small, wild – tame. **5** Teacher.

Unit 9

1 b, d, f. **2** Teacher. **3 b)** She was an actress. **c)** They had three children. **d)** Roald Dahl loved wine, chocolate, painting, music and gardening. **e)** He disliked pop songs and tripe. **f)** He reminded his teacher of a camel. **4 a)** He disliked school. **b)** He loved wine, chocolate, painting, music and gardening. **c)** "He is a persistent muddler...he reminds me of a camel."**5** * The footballer kicked the ball. * Roald Dahl is an author. * The fireman climbed the ladder. * Monkeys climb trees.

* Our teacher is kind. * The tortoise beat the hare. * Roald and Patricia had three children.

Unit 10

1 a) tunnel. **b)** capture, keep. **2 a)** stirs, chirrup, moves, leaps. **b)** chop, burn, poison, pollute. **c)** catch, leaping, trapping, stinging, hunting. **3** Horses neigh and gallop. Birds twitter and fly. Grasshoppers chirp and jump. Monkeys chatter and climb. Pigs grunt and slop. Bees buzz and sting. **4** Teacher.

Unit 11

1 a) **knocking** them to the ground and **biting** them. **b)** **swooping** towards the ground, **stunning** their prey and **tearing** it to pieces. **2 a)** move, hunt. **b)** catch, knock, stealing, eat. **c)** sit, soar, looking, eat, spot, swoop, diving, stun, carry, tear, swallow. **3 a)** laugh. **b)** soar. **c)** screech. **d)** caw. **e)** sing. **f)** tumble. **g)** slide. **h)** pounce. **i)** hunt. **j)** croak. **4** Teacher.

Unit 12

1 Put, Attach, Insert, attach, Choose, rest, sit, place, Put, count, hear, Double, write, run, count. **2** 6. **3–6** Teacher.

Unit 13

1 Teacher. **2 Verbs:** Begin, Walk, Climb, Continue, Move, Pick, Head, Travel, arrive, Walk, travelling, marked, Dig. **Adverbs:** carefully, carefully, quickly, easily, slowly, watchfully, clearly, directly. **3 b)** **slowly**, climb. **c)** **slowly**, **gently**, walk. **d)** **ferociously**, **angrily**, attack. **e)** **cunningly**, hidden. **f)** **quickly**, go. **4 a)** clearly. **b)** easily. **c)** slowly. **d)** carefully. **e)** quickly. **f)** bravely. **5** Teacher. **6 a)** angrily. **b)** dangerously. **c)** gently. **d)** frantically. **e)** silently. **f)** slowly. **g)** triumphantly.

Unit 14

1 easily. **2** carefully, slowly, neatly, legibly. **3 'how' adverbs:** quickly, firmly, slowly, carefully, gently, legibly. **'when' adverbs:** then, soon, yesterday, when, afterwards, next. **'where' adverbs:** near, here, inside, there, down, outside, up, by. **4 a)** kindly. **b)** easily. **c)** cleverly. **d)** noisily. **e)** truthfully. **f)** simply. **g)** firmly. **h)** clumsily. **i)** silently. **5** Teacher. **6** there, brightly, nearby, before, easily, when, soon, after, slowly, clearly.

Unit 15

1 a) Peta-Lyn Martin and Hilton Graham. **b)** It is about the way Peta-Lyn rescued Hilton after he was attacked. **c)** It happened in the Northern Territory. **d)** It was about midday when it happened. **2** b, d, e, f, h. **3** She saved her friend. * Peta-Lyn and Hilton were hunting wild pigs * Hilton pushed the boat. * The crocodile attacked Hilton. * It grabbed his left arm. * Peta-Lyn drove the car. * The ambulance officer treated the injured man. **4** Teacher. **5** Teacher.

Unit 16

1 For those of you who haven't heard of this, it is a day when one grade sells treats to the whole school. The treats could be cookies, muffins, fruit treats, gingerbread, slices, fruit cakes and carrot sticks. **2 a)** Healthy foods for Tuesday treats include muffins, celery sticks, apples, cheese slices, honey joys, apple cakes and pizza slices. **b)** Foods we should not bring for Tuesday Treat Day include lollies, chocolates, potato chips, sausage rolls, cream cakes and hot dogs. **3** Ingredients: cornflakes, low-fat butter, honey, coconut, sultanas. **4 a)** do the long jump, play tunnel ball and run in relays. **b)** doing the washing up, putting the rubbish out and setting the table. **c)** go to the circus, watch movies and visit the zoo. **5** The treats could be cookies, muffins, fruit treats, gingerbread, slices, fruit cake and carrot sticks.

Unit 17

2 The teacher wrote the letter to find out why Susan wasn't doing her homework. **3 b)** How – She had five brothers. **c)** Who – She needs to talk to Susan's mother. **d)** Which – She said that the dog buried Susan's homework book. **e)** Where – She goes to Mountvale Primary School. **f)** Why – She made up excuses because she hadn't done her homework. **4 a)** 'Who's that knocking on my door?" said the first little pig. **b)** "Can you tell me the way to Grandma's house?" asked the wolf. **c)** 'Who's sleeping in my bed?" wailed Goldilocks. **d)** "Mirror, mirror on the wall, who is the fairest of them all?" **e)** Jack was nimble, Jack was quick, but who jumped over the candlestick? **f)** "Who's that trip-trapping over my bridge?" roared the troll. **5** Teacher.

Unit 18

1 Don't throw the rubbish down the drain! What is the name of that tiny little bug? Some frogs have disappeared! How can we save the wetlands? What a pity! Science has proven that some animals will soon be extinct! Do you know where the litter you just threw down the drain went? When buying a plant, have you ever thought if it is native? Save the wetlands! That shouldn't be happening! Please save our wetlands! **2–5** Teacher.

Unit 19

1 it's, I'm, they're, you're, I'd, where's, I'll, I've. **2** will not, should have, did not, there is, can not, do not, you would/you had, it will. **3** can't, you'd, don't, what's, it's, I'm, there's, I'd. **4 b)** my friend's house. **c)** the horses' stables. **d)** our uncle's garden. **5 a)** birds'. **b)** king's. **c)** spiders'. **d)** fireman's. **e)** baker's. **f)** cats'. **g)** doctor's. **h)** dog's. **i)** baby's. **j)** horses'. **6** Teacher. **7 One owner** hen's, lifesaver's, teacher's, child's, bee's.

Unit 20

1 a) "Can you help me find my way home?**"** he asked a man. **b) "**Of course,**"** replied the man. **"**Follow the path straight by the tree near the river.**" 2 a) "**Help!**"** he called. **b) "**I'll grab your hands and help you down.**" 3** Teacher. **4** Teacher. **5 a)** "I'm going to beat that hare!" said the tortoise. **b)** "I want my mummy!" cried the baby. **c)** "Who stood on my tail?" screeched the cat. **6 a)** "I am lost in the jungle," said the small boy. **b)** "Shout more loudly than that," said the boy to the man. **c)** "Hooray! Well sung!" he cried as he let go of the branch.

Unit 21

1 Our blue-grey Persian cat is lost. The cat is small, very fluffy, with big, brown eyes which turn orange in the dark. **2** Teacher. **3** Teacher. **4 a)** Can you help? Have you seen her? **b)** Please help! Please return her now! **c)** Have you seen her? **d)** Please help! **e)** Have you seen her? **f)** The cat is small, very fluffy, with big, brown eyes which turn orange in the dark. **5 a)** ! **b)** ? **c)** . **d)** ! **e)** ! **f)** !! **g)** ! **h)** ? **i)** ? **j)** !. **k)** !. **l)** ! **6** Teacher.

Unit 22

1 because, and. **2** Teacher. **3 b)** Jana has a broken toe and a bruised shin. **c)** The tree crashed onto the classroom and the children ran outside. **d)** Tony shouted loudly and the teacher told him to keep quiet. **e)** Dad fell off the roof and landed on a rose bush. **4 a)** because. **b)** because. **c)** but. **d)** but. **e)** because. **f)** because. **5** Teacher. **6** while, through, until, yet, unless, that, since, because, for, although, and, but.

Unit 23

1 of, off, in, from, for, of. for, for, of. **2** through, out, over, on, through. **3** Teacher. **4 b)** off. **c)** on. **d)** down. **e)** with.

Unit 24

1 a) its journey. **b)** the body. **2 a)** by the stomach. **b)** to the small intestine. **c)** through the villi. **d)** into the large intestine. **3 a)** the oesophagus. **b)** the stomach. **c)** to the small intestine. **d)** the blood stream, the villi. **e)** the large intestine, the anus. **f)** the drain. **4 a)** in the morning. **b)** after lunch. **c)** On Monday morning. **d)** at midnight. **e)** in the morning, before dinner. **5 a)** with a great roar. **b)** in a loud voice. **c)** by the lightning flash.

Unit 25

2 b) I. **c)** Mr Fox. **d)** The fox. **e)** They. **f)** The geese. **g)** The fox. **3 b)** tricked **the fox**. **c)** said **a prayer**. **d)** took **a big breath**. **e)** saw **the geese**. **f)** has **no end**. **4** * Six horses jumped the fence. * All the geese said their prayers. * The owl opened his eyes. * The tortoise beat the hare. * The peacock shook its colourful feathers. * The eagle caught its prey. * The mouse nibbled the cheese.

Unit 26

1 a) Moth, moonshine, mean, me, Magic, madness, mystery. **b)** Witches, weird, wild. **c)** Moth, moonlit. **d)** glide, glades. **2–6** Teacher.

Unit 27

1 a) fiddle. **b)** bug, rug. **c)** bat. **d)** eel. **e)** ice. **f)** horse. **g)** stone. **h)** hyena. **2 a)** wolf. **b)** hare. **c)** tortoise. **d)** lamb. **e)** bee. **f)** fox. **3** Teacher. **4** Teacher. **Challenge** as cold as an icicle, brave as a soldier, bumble bees buzzing like high speed drills, car engine purring like a well-fed cat, thundering like a herd of elephants, as frisky as a two-year-old, sparkling like glittering jewels, as smooth as velvet, as flat as a pancake.

Unit 28

1 quack – ducks, bark – dogs, bleat (baa) – sheep, moo – cows, cock-a-doodle-doo – roosters, meow – cats, purr – cats, mo-poke – owls, hee-haw – donkeys, oink – pigs, neigh – horses. **2** washing machine. **3–6** Teacher.

Unit 29

1 bad, down, under, sad, tiny, she, loved, top, beautiful, worst, everything, take, strong, dry, above, start. **2 a)** ends. **b)** east. Teacher. **3** slow, dry, soft, below, soft, old, hate, sharp. **4 a)** unfair. **b)** incorrect. **c)** misspell. **d)** disappear. **e)** unzip. **f)** unselfish. **g)** unplug. **h)** mistake. **i)** disbelieve. **5 a)** unkind. **b)** dislike. **c)** misbehave. **d)** unwell. **6** mustn't, doesn't, haven't. **7 a)** up. **b)** hairy. **c)** after. **d)** rich. **e)** hard. **f)** full. **g)** good. **h)** worse. **i)** sick. **Mystery word:** pitchfork.

Unit 30

1 a) like, love. **b)** write, jot, write. **c)** note, letter. **d)** finish, stop. **2** Teacher. **3 Across:** 1 stop. 3 like. 4 good. 5 help. 6 animals. 7 heaps. 8 rubbish. 9 care. 10 away. 11 write. 12 chosen. 13 lunch. **Down:** 1 save. 2 pick. 3 letter. 9 closing. 14 want.

2 **Sentences must make sense. Tick the groups of words which are sentences. Circle the full stops and a draw a square around the capital letters. What do you notice?**

____

a is a heroine ☐
b The crocodile attacked him. ☐
c lost an enormous amount ☐
d I had a firm grip on his arm. ☐
e He quickly lost consciousness. ☐
f She dragged him to the river bank. ☐
g their boat ☐
h Their boat got stuck. ☐

3 **Make complete sentences by joining the subject, verb and object. (The first one is done for you.)**

Subject	Verb	Object
A young girl	became	her friend
She	attacked	a heroine
Peta-Lyn and Hilton	grabbed	Hilton
Hilton	pushed	wild pigs
The crocodile	were hunting	the injured man
It	treated	the boat
Peta-Lyn	drove	his left arm
The ambulance officer	saved	the car

4 **Make your own headlines. In the headline below, *Young girl* is the subject, *fights* is the verb and *crocodile* is the object.**

Young girl fights crocodile

5 **In the headlines below, circle the subject (who or what the sentence is about), highlight the verb (the doing word) and underline the object (who or what the subject does something to).**

Girl saves pighunter

Huge croc attacks tin boat

Hunter survives monster attack

Challenge!

On a separate page, make up some eye-catching headlines of your own.

Your turn to write

Make up a newspaper report about something exciting, interesting or heroic that you have seen. Gather the facts first. Think of a good headline. Present the most important details in the first paragraph. Tell who, when, what, where. Make sure the report has paragraphs and that each sentence makes sense.

Commas

Commas indicate a pause shorter than for a full stop.

Commas mark a pause in a sentence.

Commas separate items in a list.

Mountvale Primary School

Newsletter 14 March 2008

Title of transaction

Introducing Tuesday Treats

Introduction

NOTICE for parents, grandparents, children and school community members.

General description
To indicate purpose

You might remember the well-known Mountvale PS "Friday Feast Day". Since we have canteen on Friday, we had to move our treat day to Tuesday.

For those of you who haven't heard of this, it is a day when one grade sells treats to the whole school. The treats could be cookies, muffins, fruit treats, gingerbread, slices, fruit cakes and carrot sticks.

Details of transaction

All the treats are sold for 50 cents each.

It is best if the treats are home-made and also healthy. They should be brought to school in an environmentally friendly, airtight container.

Remember, each item is 50 cents.

First Tuesday Treat Day, coming up. Tuesday 27 March. Grade 4. Be there!

Seeking response from others

10 % of the money we raise goes to charity. Remember: healthy food, please.

Concluding statement

We hope that you enjoy Tuesday Treat days.

Erin, Grade 4L

1 Cover the newsletter text above. A paragraph from the text is below, but the commas have been left out. Write in the missing commas, then check to see if you have put them in the correct places.

For those of you who haven't heard of this it is a day when one grade sells treats to the whole school. The treats could be cookies muffins fruit treats gingerbread slices fruit cakes and carrot sticks.

Explain to the students that when listing words we use a comma instead of the word *and*, except between the last two items in a list.
Talk about the structure of a transaction. Transactions usually involve some form of negotiation. The information is presented in a precise, logical and sequential form.

Comma

A comma shows a short break or a pause in a sentence, for example, *She decided to stop, even though she was late.*

Commas are also used to separate lists, for example, *The ingredients used for apricot jam are apricots, sugar, pectin and water*

2 Insert commas where they are needed.

a Healthy foods for Tuesday treats include muffins celery sticks apples cheese slices honey joys apple cakes and pizza slices.

b Foods we should not bring for Tuesday Treat Day include lollies chocolates potato chips sausage rolls cream cakes and hot dogs.

3 Put the commas in the correct places on the label.

Honey Joys
Ingredients: cornflakes low-fat butter honey coconut sultanas.

4 Complete the sentences by using three or four groups of words from the box. (Use up all of the words.)

do the long jump	make food for treats	setting the table	visit the zoo
putting the rubbish out	go to the circus	watch movies	run in relays
doing the washing up	play tunnel ball		

a At school sport we ______________________________

____

b I help mum by ______________________________

____

c When I go out, I like to ______________________________

____

5 Look again at the transaction opposite. Write a sentence listing some of the treats.

____

____

Think of a special way that you or your class could raise money for your school or a charity. Then, as a group or on your own, write up your idea. Include a heading or title for your idea. Write a description and use headings and pictures to give more details about your idea. Check to see if your grade and teacher like your idea. If it works, you could present it in the school newsletter.

Questions

A question mark is used at the end of a sentence.

Why Hasn't Susan Done Her Homework?

14 March 2008

Mary Simpson
Mountvale P.S.
Mountain Road
Mountvale 3765

Dear Mrs Johnson

I am writing this letter because all week I have been asking your daughter, Susan, for her homework. Each time I asked her, she had a different reason for not doing her work. Could you please let me know whether her excuses are true or made up?

These are the questions I need answering:

Did her baby sister eat her spelling on Monday?
Did you post her project to her grandmother by mistake?
Did the dog bury her maths book in the back yard?
Did her father use her dictation book to light the fire?

Could you please respond as soon as possible.

Yours sincerely,

Mary Simpson

(Susan's teacher)

question mark

question mark

Date

Address

Introduction or greeting

Description To indicate purpose

Details Information and questions for the reader

Final statement

Signature of the sender

Dear Mrs Simpson

It seems that Susan is a big story teller. This is why.

- She has five brothers, but no sister, so the baby sister couldn't have eaten the homework.
- She doesn't have a grandmother, just two grandfathers.
- We have two cats and a rabbit, but no dog, so how could it bury the homework?
- We have central heating and no open fire, so how could the dictation book be burnt?

I think that Susan and I need to have a little talk about her homework. I will ask her these questions:

- Why do you make up stories?
- Why don't you do your homework?

Could you please let me know if she makes any more excuses.

Yours sincerely,

Tracey Johnson

1 Highlight all the sentences which are questions. (You should find nine.)

2 Write the answer to this question. Why did the teacher write the letter?

Revise the purpose of a transaction (to conduct an exchange involving some form of interaction). Look at the different forms of interaction above: the formal letter and the informal note in reply. See how the purpose of the letter is to seek information.

Unit 17

Question mark

The question mark is used at the end of a sentence which asks a question.

Question words

Who Why Where When Which How What

3 Look again at the letter and note opposite. Then choose the most suitable word from the question word list to begin each sentence below, and write a short answer for each question. (The first is done for you.)

a ___What___ did Susan say her baby sister did? ___Susan said that her baby sister ate her homework.___

b ____________ many brothers did she have? ____________

c ____________ does Mrs Simpson need to talk to? ____________

d ____________ book did she say that the dog buried? ____________

e ____________ does Susan go to school? ____________

f ____________ did Susan make up excuses? ____________

4 Add question marks, full stops, commas and capital letters to these sentences.

a "who's that knocking on my door " said the first little pig

b "can you tell me the way to Grandma's house " asked the wolf

c "who's sleeping in my bed " wailed goldilocks

d "mirror mirror on the wall who is the fairest of them all "

e jack was nimble jack was quick but who jumped over the candlestick

f "who's that trip-trapping over my bridge " roared the troll

5 Write a question beginning with each question word.

a Whose ____________

b Did ____________

c Why ____________

d How ____________

e If ____________

f Where ____________

You have been appointed to find out the answers to the questions which are the most important to the students in your classroom. Conduct a survey. Find out the questions that the students really want to ask. Then write a letter to your teacher asking him or her to try to provide answers to the questions.

Exclamations

Exclamations

Exclamations are words which show strong feelings.

Draw a box around all the exclamations in this text.

Wetland World

Title

Wetlands are some of the world's most wonderful places. Unfortunately, they're getting destroyed. That shouldn't be happening!

Statement of position A point of view

Wetlands hold many lovely animals, but the lovely animals I'm talking about, such as platypuses, frogs, fishes and those tiny little bugs that we never remember the names of, will soon be extinct. Science has proven that!

Arguments 1 Supporting the point of view

Do you know where that litter you just threw down the drain went? What a pity! That drain goes into the stormwater pipes which lead to wetlands, creeks, lakes and oceans, and your piece is one of many pieces of rubbish that choke animals.

2

When buying a plant, have you ever thought if it is native? If you don't, you could be buying a weed. Yes, the weed that takes over your garden and kills your best plants can get into the wetlands too!

3

I have said all I have to say. Please save our wetlands!

Carlie, Grade 4L

Concluding statement

Exclamation marks

Exclamation marks look like this: !
They are used in writing to show strong feelings.

Read the text and do the activities.

1 **The questions and exclamations have all been mixed up. Put the marks in the correct places. Refer back to the exposition if you need to.**

Don't throw rubbish down the drain ◯

What is the name of that tiny little bug ◯

Some frogs have disappeared ◯

How can we save the wetlands ◯

What a pity ◯

Science has proven that some animals will soon be extinct ◯

Do you know where the litter you just threw down the drain went ◯

When buying a plant, have you ever thought if it is native ◯

Save the wetlands ◯

That shouldn't be happening ◯

Please save our wetlands ◯

Discuss the structure of an exposition. Talk about the need to express feelings strongly when arguing a point of view. Demonstrate how the exclamation may play an important part in expository writing.

Exclamation

If you exclaim, it means that you call out suddenly.
Exclamation marks are used to show this in writing.

2 What are the people exclaiming?
Write a suitable exclamation in each speech bubble.

3 Below are some exclamations. Draw suitable cartoons and speech bubbles for them. (You will need to make the cartoons small.)

Watch out!	Who goes there!	Save the frog!	It's a boy!

4 Write your own sentence to follow each exclamation.

a Stop, thief! __________

b Pull over, driver! __________

5 Write an exclamation that you might shout, instead of saying these long sentences. Use only one or two words.

a Please finish your writing immediately. __________

b I heard you knocking at the door, so you can enter. __________

c I think I see a large shark swimming our way. __________

How do you feel about the way people are damaging our world? How can we prevent more animals from becoming extinct? Write your opinion and then provide some arguments to support what you say. Include some drawings or cartoons to support your case.

Apostrophes

An apostrophe is used to show where a word is shortened.

it's = it is

what's = what is

don't = do not

I'm = I am

The City Is Better

← Title

I enjoy living in the city. It's great to be in a place where there are lots of people.

← Statement of position

Time goes quickly in the city because there's always something happening. It's easy to get to places because trams, trains and buses are everywhere. It's easier to visit your friends and relations and what's more, the shopping is so colourful and exciting.

← *Argument 1*

I'm sure that the country is very exciting, but I can't see what you'd do there all day. I don't understand what's so great about cows and rabbits and all those farm things.

← *Argument 2*

Worst of all, I'd hate to think that one day a farm animal might be your friend and the next day it might end up on your dinner plate.

← *Argument 3*

All things considered, I'm glad I live in the city. I don't ever want to change to the country. That's the truth!

← **Concluding statement** To reinforce the position taken

Apostrophes

The apostrophe of contraction is used to show when one or more letters are left out of a word. For example, *I am = I'm*

1 Write the contractions for these words.

it is ______ I am ______ they are ______ you are ______

I would ______ where is ______ I will ______ I have ______

2 Write out the contractions in full.

won't ______ should've ______ didn't ______ there's ______

can't ______ don't ______ you'd ______ it'll ______

3 Look again at the exposition. Highlight the contractions for these words when you find them and write them in the spaces.

cannot ______ you would ______ do not ______ what is ______

it is ______ I am ______ there is ______ I would ______

Look again at the elements of an exposition. Focus on the opening statement. Stress the importance of putting your point of view strongly at the beginning, and then supporting that statement with arguments.

Talk about apostrophes of contraction and possession.

Apostrophes

The apostrophe of possession is used to show ownership.
For example, *the boy's bike* (the bike belonging to the boy)
the cat's whiskers (the whiskers of the cat)
BUT, if there is more than one, we add the apostrophe after the 's'.
For example, *the cats' whiskers*

4 Rewrite the phrases using an apostrophe. (The first one is done for you.)

a the paddock of the bull ___the bull's paddock___

b the house of my friend ______

c the stables of the horses ______

d the garden of our uncle ______

5 The owners are in the box. Match them to the most suitable things below.

spiders'	king's	fireman's	baby's	birds'
cats'	doctor's	horses'	baker's	dog's

a The ______ nests

b The ______ crown

c The ______ webs

d The ______ ladder

e The ______ bread

f The ______ whiskers

g The ______ stethoscope

h The ______ kennel

i The ______ pram

j The ______ stables

6 Write the words in sentences.

a doctors' ______

b nurse's ______

c aunt's ______

7 Tick the boxes if the word shows one owner. Write a cross if it shows more than one owner.

tigers' ☐ hen's ☐ lifesaver's ☐

skiers' ☐ teacher's ☐ eagles' ☐

teenagers' ☐ child's ☐ bee's ☐

spider's web
(one spider)

spiders' webs
(more than one spider)

Your turn to write

The city or the country? Write your point of view. Which do you think is better? Make sure you include some good arguments to support your preference.

Grammar focus

Quotation marks

Narrative structure

Quotation marks

Quotation marks are sometimes called speech marks.

The Silly Boy

Once, in India, a small boy was lost. "Can you help me find my way home?" he asked a man. "Of course," replied the man. "Follow the path straight by the tree near the river."

The silly boy raced along the path and ran straight up the tree. Up, up, to the very top branch. CRACK! It broke. Luckily, he fell down onto a low branch.

"Help!" he called.

Along came a driver on an elephant. "Hang on!" he cried. "I'll grab your hands and help you down."

He leaned across and caught the silly boy's hands, but the elephant took fright and ran away.

So there they were, dangling over the rushing river. "Help! Help!" they cried. "Sing out more loudly," cried the boy. The elephant driver sang out even more loudly. "Hooray! Well sung!" cried the silly boy, clapping his hands.

Of course they both fell into the deep river below. Splash! And it's a wonder they both didn't drown.

An Indian folktale

Quotation marks show the beginning and the end of the words spoken.

Title

Orientation Where? Who? What?

Complication (Something unexpected happens)

Sequence of events

Resolution and concluding comment

Read the narrative and do the activities.

1 **Read the orientation and then place the quotation marks in the correct places.**

a Can you help me find my way home? he asked a man.

b Of course, replied the man. Follow the path straight by the tree near the river.

2 **Read the sequence of events and then answer the questions.**

a What did the boy call out when he fell onto a low branch?

____

b What did the elephant driver say?

____

3 **Look at the second last paragraph. Circle all the quotation marks. Highlight all the words which are spoken.**

Don't forget to put in the quotation marks.

To the teacher

Discuss quotation marks. Sometimes single quotation marks are used to indicate speech, for example, *'Hang on!' he said*. Sometimes double quotation marks are used: *"Help!" he called*. Revise the features of a narrative. Note that direct speech is often included in narrative texts.

Quotation marks

"When do we use quotation marks?" barked the teacher.

"We use them to show the exact words that someone has spoken," replied the child.

4 Change the sentences into pictures with speech bubbles.

"Hang on!" cried the elephant driver.

"Help!" yelled the boy.

"Hooray! Well sung!" cried the boy, clapping his hands.

5 Change these cartoons into sentences.

I'm going to beat that hare.

I want my mummy.

______________________________ ______________________________ ______________________________

______________________________ ______________________________ ______________________________

______________________________ ______________________________ ______________________________

6 Write quotation marks where they belong in these sentences.

a I am lost in the jungle, said the small boy.

b Shout more loudly than that, said the boy to the man.

c Hooray! Well sung! he cried as he let go of the branch.

Create your own comic strip. Tell the story of the silly boy through pictures and speech bubbles. Remember: your first picture will show what happens in the orientation and the last picture will show what happens in the resolution.

Sentences

Sentences always begin with a capital letter.

They can end with either:

a full stop (.)

an exclamation mark (!)

or a question mark (?).

Missing!

Please return her now!

Our blue-grey Persian cat is lost. Can you help?

Her owner says:
"She is very timid and will run away when strangers approach. Please don't chase her. I'm afraid she might run onto the road and get hit."

The cat is small, very fluffy, with big, brown eyes which turn orange in the dark.

Please help!

Have you seen her?
We will pay a big
REWARD for her return.

Contact this number: 07 675 5084
Address: Bluehills Road,
Richmond, Tasmania 6704

Read the poster and do the activities.

1 **Underline two sentences in the poster which begin with a capital letter and end with a full stop. (They describe the cat.)**

2 **Write a sentence of your own which has:**

a more than ten words ______________________________

____

b three words or less. ______________________________

____

3 **Colour a sentence which contains the words the owner says about her cat. Find the quotation marks in this sentence and circle them.**

Expository or persuasive texts can take the form of an advertisement or poster. They often feature repetition of words, slogans or catchy sayings, questions that appeal to the reader and exclamations which capture attention.

4 Look at the poster and write:

a two sentences which are questions

____

____

b two sentences which are exclamations

____

____

c a sentence of four words

____

d a sentence of only two words

____

e a sentence of four words and a question mark

____

f a sentence which contains a capital letter, three commas and a full stop.

____

5 Complete these sentences with a question mark, full stop or exclamation mark.

a Put your pens down now

b Will you be here soon

c Everyone can go out to play

d Children at the back, sing up

e I like Phys. Ed.

f Keep walking Don't stop

g Quick, the train's coming

h What's for lunch

i Can you hear the whisper

j Everybody back inside It's a wet day timetable

k Hurry up It's time for art

l Who likes maths

6 Make up your own sentences using these endings.

a ______________________________ asked the teacher, looking at her watch.

b ______________________________ in the compost bin.

c ______________________________ swim for the shore!

d ______________________________ on the Easter Break?

e ______________________________ shouted the principal.

Your turn to write

Design a poster or an advertisement connected to a topic you are working on in the classroom. Include in your poster: a question or a statement in bold letters saying what the poster is about; some catchy slogans or rhymes; some questions that would appeal to the reader; an exclamation in bold lettering; a picture, diagram or sketch; a reward or an offer.

Conjunctions

Conjunctions are joining words.

Why Do We Have a Skeleton?

Question in heading

A skeleton is made up of many bones. These bones provide a framework, or a way of keeping the whole body together.

Identifying statement Tells us about the topic to be explained

We need the skeleton because without it we would not be supported and we would just flop about like a rag doll.

conjunctions

The skeleton provides us with a kind of a cage which helps to protect our heart, lungs and brain.

Explanation sequence A series of points telling how and why

The skeleton also has a system of levers or moving parts that the muscles can use to help us to walk, sit and run.

conjunction

skull
collar-bone
breastbone
rib
backbone

Diagram Explanations often have diagrams

So the skeleton is needed to enable us to perform all the movements necessary for a healthy life.

Conclusion (Rounding off sentence)

A conjunction is used to connect words or groups of words. The most common conjunctions are *and*, *but* and *because*.

Read the explanation and do the activities.

1 Two joining words or conjunctions have been left out. Fill the gaps.

We need the skeleton ____________________ without it we would not be supported

____________________ we would just flop about like a rag doll.

2 Write these joining words in sentences of your own.

a and ____________________

b but ____________________

c or ____________________

d because ____________________

A feature of the explanation is the sequence in which the link between cause and effect is presented. Conjunctions such as *if*, *then* and *because* are often used in these explanation sequences. At this level, focus first on the most commonly used conjunctions—*and*, *but*, *because*—before introducing the expanded list. (See Question 5 opposite.)

3 **Use the conjunction *and* to join a sentence from the first box to a sentence from the second box. (The first one is done for you.)**

The train pulled into the station.	The children ran outside.
Jana has a broken toe.	Dad landed on a rose bush.
The tree crashed onto the classroom.	The passengers jumped on board.
Tony shouted loudly.	Jana has a bruised shin.
Dad fell off the roof.	The teacher told him to keep quiet.

a The train pulled into the station and the passengers jumped on board.

b ______________________________

c ______________________________

d ______________________________

e ______________________________

4 **Which conjunction is correct: *but* or *because*? Circle the correct word in each sentence.**

a It is good to exercise because / but it keeps you fit.

b Bones are important because / but they keep the body together.

c We have many ribs because / but only one spine.

d Bones sometimes break because / but they usually heal quickly.

e The skull is very important because / but it protects the brain.

f We need the skeleton because / but without it we would flop about like a rag doll.

5 **Tick each conjunction in the box when you have found it in the word search.**

although	and	because	but
for	since	that	through
unless	until	while	yet

S	O	C	F	W	G	P	A	T	S
T	E	T	K	W	E	L	L	H	I
Q	T	U	B	J	T	S	H	R	N
T	S	B	B	H	S	T	R	O	C
D	J	T	O	E	Z	O	R	U	E
H	Q	U	L	I	F	Z	U	G	C
I	G	N	E	L	I	H	W	H	U
H	U	L	I	T	N	U	Y	C	J
T	A	H	T	D	N	A	H	E	X
Y	E	S	U	A	C	E	B	G	T

6 **The vowels of these conjunctions have been left out. Write them in.**

wh__l__	thr____gh	__nt__l	y__t
__nl__ss	th__t	s__nc__	b__c____s__
f__r	__lth____gh	__nd	b__t

Your turn to write

Choose one of these two topics and write an explanation: 'How birds make their nests' or 'How bees make honey'. Divide your explanation into these parts: question in heading; identifying statement (telling how and why); diagram; concluding statement (rounding off).

Prepositions

What Can We Do to …

Save the Planet?

Question in heading

preposition
noun

In a very short space of time we have polluted the Earth. Here's how we can save it.

Identifying statement
Introduces what is being explained

Recycle rubbish.

Explanation sequence
Explains how we can save the planet

Become waste watchers

- Re-use and mend as many things as we can.
- Recycle our rubbish.
- Turn off those lights.

preposition
noun

Use water wisely.

Become clean and green

- Turn down the heater and the air conditioner in our classrooms.
- Use wind power to cool and sun power to warm.

Stop pollution

- Walk to school if it is not too far away.
- Use a bike to get from one place to another.

Don't pollute.

Buy wisely

- Think before you buy.
- Choose products which are good for the environment.

preposition
noun

If we think about how we act, then every one of us can help to make our planet sustainable so that it will be a better place for us and for all the people of the future.

Think about the ozone layer.

Concluding statement
The end result

A preposition is a word put in front of a noun or pronoun to show how the noun or pronoun is connected with another word.

Read the poster and do the activities.

1. **The words *of, off, to, in, from, for* are all prepositions. Use your highlighter to colour these prepositions when you see them in the explanation above.**

This explanation is presented in the form of a poster. Discuss the features of an explanation. Prepositions show the connection between the noun and the other words in a sentence. They are usually placed before the nouns. Identify with the students the prepositions and nouns in the explanation above.

Prepositions

above	across	along	around	among	against	after	before
behind	below	beneath	between	beside	in	into	on
onto	by	at	to	up	upon	down	through
off	under	over	with	within	without	near	far

2 The sentences below are all about a boy running in the obstacle race. Fill the gaps with the correct prepositions.

First he ran ________________ the gate with the 'in' sign. Next he ran ________________ the other side. Then he jumped ________________ the hurdle. Next he came to a pipe which was ________________ some sand. He went ________________ the pipe and came out the other side.

3 Write a sentence for each preposition and noun pair, for example, *near / car*: Gemma was not near the car.

a at / home ________________

b from / school ________________

c across / road ________________

d beside / pond ________________

e over / bridge ________________

f between / trees ________________

4 The prepositions are in bold. Write the opposite preposition above the bold one. (The first one is done for you.)

a Sal walked over **under** the bridge. (over)

b Lila jumped **on** the train.

c Con climbed **off** the monkey bars.

d The campers drove **up** the mountain.

e My mother left the shops **without** her wallet.

You have been asked to invent a way that people can save water. Draw your invention and write an explanation.

Phrases

Phrases
Phrases are groups of words without verbs.

Where Does a Snail Go When It Is Eaten?

Title
Question in heading

When a snail gets eaten, lots of things happen on its journey through the body.

phrase → on its journey

General statement

First, the snail gets chewed up. Then the saliva (spit) helps break it down. The snail screams, "Help! I'm being eaten." It goes down the oesophagus into the stomach and screams, "Help! I'm being eaten. Digested! Yuk!" It gets broken down by the stomach acid and screams, "Help! I'm being attacked by acid." Then it gets pushed down to the small intestine.

The healthy bits go into the blood stream through the villi, the small hairs in the small intestine. The un-useful parts go into the large intestine, through the anus (or backside).

Explanation sequence
In the explanation sequence technical words are used, e.g. *saliva*, *oesophagus*, *villi*, *intestine*, *anus*.

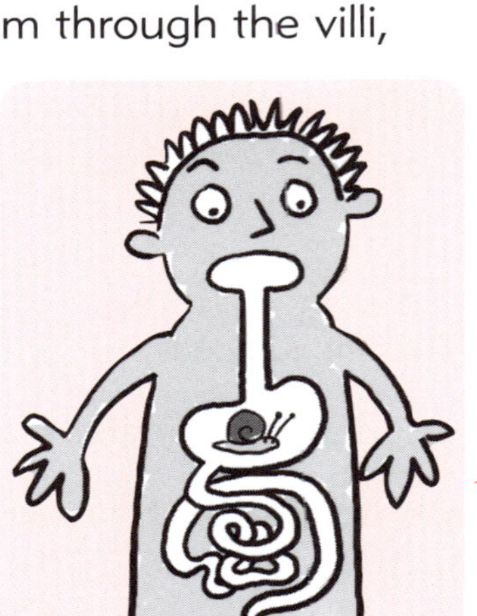

Finally, what's left of the snail screams, "Help! I'm being flushed round the S-bend and down the drain."

phrase → of the snail

So that's what happens to the snail and lots of other food when it gets eaten.

Concluding statement
Summing up

by Dylan (Gr. 4)

Phrases

A phrase is a group of words without a verb. It is used to make sentences more interesting. Most phrases begin with a preposition.

Read the explanation and do the activities.

1 Write phrases from the general statement beginning with these prepositions.

a on ________________ ______________________ **b** through ________________ ____________________

2 Write phrases from the explanation sequence beginning with these prepositions.

a by ______________________ ______________________

b to ____________________ ____________________ ____________________

c through ______________________ ______________________

d into ____________________ ____________________ ____________________

Challenge!
After you have written the phrases, highlight them in the explanation.

Before discussing phrases, look again at Prepositions (Unit 23). Since phrases usually begin with prepositions, identify the prepositions in the text and then identify the whole phrase. The students could circle the prepositions and highlight the phrases.
Look again at the structure of explanations. Discuss the use of technical language in the text.

Adverbial phrases

An adverbial phrase tells us more about an action. It can tell us where, when or how an action is done.

Remember:

- phrases do not contain a verb
- phrases often begin with a preposition.

Example of an adverbial phrase:
The food goes down the oesophagus.
'down the oesophagus' is a phrase telling where the food goes.

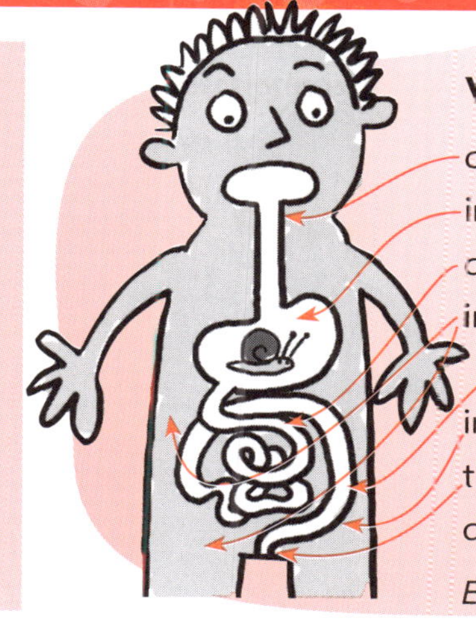

Where does food go?

down the oesophagus
into the stomach
down to the small intestine
into the bloodstream
through the villi
into the large intestine
through the anus
down the drain

Explanation by Dylan

3 Complete the sentences with adverbial phrases telling 'where'. (The diagram and labels above will help with your answers.)

a After the food is chewed it goes **down** ____________________

b It travels from the oesophagus **into** ____________________

c The food gets pushed **down** ____________________

d The healthy bits go **into** ____________________ **through** ____________________

e The unhealthy bits go **into** ____________________ and then **through** ____________________

f The waste ends up being flushed round the S-bend and **down** ____________________

4 Underline the adverbial phrase which tells 'when' in each sentence.

a We do our athletics training in the morning.

b I usually eat fruit after lunch.

c On Monday morning we have assembly.

d The possum fell down the chimney at midnight.

e We started in the morning and arrived just before dinner.

Phrases can be at the end, in the middle or at the beginning of sentences.

5 Complete the sentences using an adverbial phrase telling 'how' from the box.

in a loud voice	with a great roar	by the lightning flash

a The fire swept through the forest ____________________

b The headmaster spoke ____________________

c The whole sky was lit up ____________________

As a class, decide which things about the body you would like explained. For example, 'Where does food go?' Research one of these questions and in groups, present the explanations to the rest of the class.

Clauses

A main clause makes sense on its own.

clause

Most main clauses contain:

a subject (He)

a verb (saw)

an object (seven fat geese).

A subordinate clause does not make sense on its own.

A Story with No End

The fox was always hungry. One day he decided to find some food. He crept out of the wood. He saw seven fat geese. They were sitting all in a row in a green field. "I will eat them," he thought to himself.

"Good morning, my dears," he said to the geese. "What a fine lunch you will make. It's no use trying to run away, for I am going to eat you, one by one."

Then he grinned a wicked grin, and licked his lips with his long, red tongue.

The geese were very worried, and began to look the picture of sadness. But at last one of them spoke up boldly. "If you are going to eat us up, Mr Fox, will you grant us one last wish?"

"What is that?" asked the fox.

"Let us say our prayers. Let us pray to the god of all geese. We will beg our god to forgive our sins, and after that we will die happy."

"Very well," said the fox, who liked to pretend he was very kind, even though everyone knew how wicked he really was. "Begin your prayers now, and I promise that I won't touch a feather of your necks until you have finished."

So the first goose began to pray. "Gabble-gabble," it said. "Gabble-gabble-gabble."

Then the second one looked up into the blue sky and said, "Gabble-gabble."

The third one began in the same way.

Each one of the seven geese looked up in the sky and began to say its prayers.

On and on they went, and if one stopped to take a breath, another started.

And if the geese had ever stopped saying their prayers, this story might have had an end. But to tell you the truth, those geese have never stopped gabbling.

Perhaps they never will.

Clauses A clause is a group of words that tell us about an action and the people or things involved in that action.

Read the narrative and do the activities.

1 Look at the narrative again. Highlight the clause, 'He saw seven fat geese.'

This clause has:

- a subject—*He* (The subject is the person or thing doing the action.)
- a verb—*saw* (*saw* is the action word or verb.)
- an object—*seven fat geese* (The object is the person or thing receiving the action of the verb.)

When looking for the subject, ask yourself who or what is doing the action.

Look again at Units 9 and 15 which introduce the concepts of subject, verb and object. Talk about this narrative. Why does this narrative not really have a resolution?

2 Underline the subject of each clause. (The first one is done for you.)

a He saw seven fat geese.

b I will eat them.

c Mr Fox granted one last wish.

d The fox licked his lips.

e They said their prayers.

f The geese tricked the fox.

g The fox liked fat geese.

3 Underline the object in each clause and place a square around the verb. (The first one is done for you.)

a The fox licked his lips.

b The first goose tricked the fox.

c The second goose said a prayer.

d The third goose took a big breath.

e The fox saw the geese.

f This story has no end.

4 Use arrows to connect the subject with its verb and object. (Each clause must make sense.) The first is done for you.

Subject	Verb	Object
The fox	beat	his eyes
Six horses	liked	the fence
All the geese	opened	its prey
The owl	said	fat geese
The tortoise	jumped	the hare
The peacock	caught	their prayers
The eagle	nibbled	its colourful feathers
The mouse	shook	the cheese

Write a story. It must contain an orientation (which tells who, what, where and when); three paragraphs (in the first paragraph, something different or unusual happens which changes the direction of the story); and a resolution (the complication must be resolved).

In 'A story with no end' there was no resolution because the geese never stopped gabbling.

Alliteration

Alliteration is the use of the same sound at the beginning of words.

Moths and Moonshine

Moths and moonshine mean to me
Magic—madness—mystery.

Witches dancing weird and wild
Mischief make for man and child.

Owls screech from woodland shades,
Moths glide through moonlit glades.

Moving in dark and secret wise
Like a plotter in disguise.

Moths and moonshine mean to me
Magic—madness—mystery.

James Reeves

alliteration → W, w, w

Title

Verses
Two-line verses. These verses are called couplets (couple = 2). The words in each couplet rhyme.

Poet

Read the poem and do the activities.

1 Find words in the poem which begin with the same sound.

a In Verse 1, find seven words beginning with 'm'. ______ ______ ______ ______ ______ ______ ______

b In Verse 2, find three words beginning with 'w'.

______ ______ ______

c In Verse 3, find two words beginning with 'm'.

______ ______

d In Verse 3, find two words beginning with 'g'.

______ ______

2 Colour code the alliteration.

a Colour the 'm' sounds red. b Colour the 'w' sounds blue. c Colour the 'g' sounds green.

3 Tongue-twisters are a form of alliteration. Try saying these five times faster than usual.

a She sells sea shells by the sea shore.
b Shun summer sunshine.
c Rush the washing Russell.
d Six split spatulas

Not all words in alliteration begin with the same letter. For example, "Once the wild wind blows". In this case the letter 'o' makes the 'w' sound.

Alliteration

Alliteration often sounds pleasant. It often adds to the meaning of the poet's words. For example:
"short, sharp, shiny"
"the simmering summer sun"
"sleep, my little one, sleep my pretty one, sleep".

4 Write your own 'number' alliterations. (The first one is done for you.)

a five Five fit fellows fixed favourite foods for fifty-five fighters.

b six ______

c nine ______

d two ______

5 Often advertisers write catchy titles or slogans using alliteration. In the advertisements below, use alliterative words to catch the reader's attention. The first one is done for you.

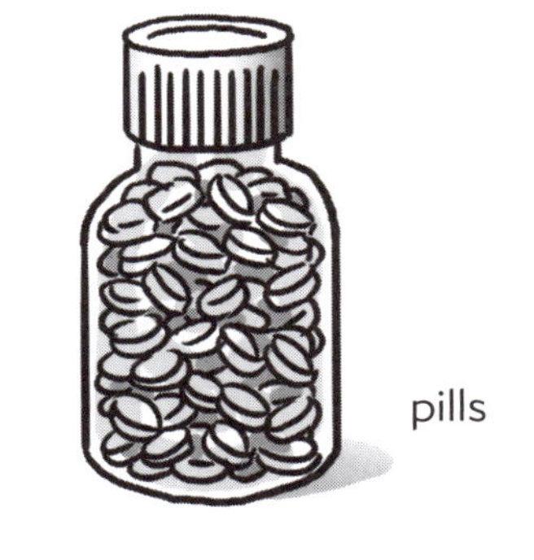

pills

Pete's peppy potions and pills.

Priceless value

______

cones

______

______

______

mobiles

______

______

______

Your turn to write

Grandad lost something beginning with "T"
A toffee?
Or a teapot or even a tie?
"A tuba?" I said
"Or some treacle?"
Or a tray or a ticket,
A tree or a thicket
A thistle, a tape, a tack?
James Reeves

In this verse, at the very end, Grandad remembered that he'd lost his temper, so he gave the boy a 'whack'.

Write your own verse.
Someone lost something beginning with …
(Your choice of letter)

______

______

______

______

______

______

Mum's Hair Dryer

It whizzes and whooshes
and buzzes at me
It sounds much more like
a bad tempered bee.

by Maggie Holmes

similes

A simile is when you compare one thing with another. Maggie thinks her mum's hairdryer sounds like a bad-tempered bee.

"Like a bad-tempered bee" is a simile.

A simile is always introduced by the words *as* or *like*.

1 Here are some well-known similes. See if you can finish them quickly. (The clues are around the border.)

horse
ice

a He was as fit as a ________________.

b The baby was as snug as a ________________ in a ________________.

c Grandpa was as blind as a ________________.

d She was as slippery as an ________________.

e It was as cold as ________________.

f He ate like a ________________.

g It dropped like a ________________.

h He laughed like a ________________.

fiddle

bug in a rug

eel
bat

stone

hyena

2 Underline the best word to complete the simile.

a	as hungry as a	circus	wolf	caterpillar	ghost	dove
b	as fast as a	tortoise	dingo	hare	elephant	stone
c	as slow as a	giant	bulldog	judge	tortoise	dog
d	as gentle as a	lamb	turkey	daisy	thief	pig
e	as busy as a	butter	cucumber	clock	gazelle	bee
f	as cunning as a	donkey	fox	cow	ant	swan

3 These similes begin with *like*. Write each ending.

a The boy swam like ______________________

b She ran like the ______________________

c His eyes shone like ______________________

d They climbed the tree like ______________________

e The pool of water shone like ______________________

4 These similes begin with *as*. Write each ending.

a The baby's curly, wispy hair is as soft as ______________________

b My dad's whiskers are as scratchy as ______________________

c The shark's skin is as rough as ______________________

d The elephant's footsteps are as loud as ______________________

e The school bag is as heavy as ______________________

Challenge!

These similes have all been mixed up. Join the simile to its correct beginning by using arrows.

baby faces wobble	like a well-fed cat
as cold	as a pancake
brave	like jelly
bumble bees buzzing	as a two-year-old child
car engine purring	as an icicle
thundering	like high speed drills
as frisky	as velvet
sparkling	as a soldier
as smooth	like a herd of elephants
as flat	like glittering jewels

To the teacher

In 'Challenge!', the similes using *like* were written by poets. They show how writing can be enlivened by similes. Discuss them with the students before they try to write their own.

Your turn to write

Here are three similes by poets.

- "Sun shines like burning honey"
- "A house without children is like a tree without birds"
- "teeth like razor-sharp daggers"

On another page, write similes for:

- an elephant's ears
- the waves crashing
- a lamb
- a lion's roar
- raindrops
- the vacuum cleaner.

Don't forget to use the words *as* or *like* in your similes.

Onomatopoeia

Some words help us to hear the sounds that are made by things.

On the Ning Nang Nong

← Title

On the Ning Nang Nong
Where the cows go Bong!
And the monkeys all say Boo!
There's a Nong Nang Ning
Where the trees go Ping!
And the teapots Jibber Jabber Joo
On the Nong Ning Nang
All the mice go Clang!
And you just can't catch 'em when they do
So it's Ning Nang Nong!

← Verse

Fill in the missing words of the chorus.

Cows go ____ ____ ____ ____
Nong Nang ____ ____ ____ ____
Trees go ____ ____ ____ ____
Nong Ning ____ ____ ____ ____
The mice go Clang!
What a noisy place to belong,
Is the Ning ____ ____ ____ ____ Ning ____ ____ ____ ____ Nong!!

Spike Milligan

← Poet

Onomatopoeia Onomatopoeia (pronounced *on-uh-mat-uh-pee-yuh*) means 'words that imitate sounds'.

Read the poem with your teacher, then do the activities.

1 These sounds are easy. Fill the gaps.

Name the animals that…

quack ____________________

bleat (baa) ____________________

cock-a-doodle-do ____________________

purr ____________________

hee-haw ____________________

neigh ____________________

bark ____________________

moo ____________________

mee-ow ____________________

mo-poke ____________________

oink ____________________

2 Something in the laundry has broken down. Read the verse below, listen to the sounds and answer the puzzle.

Racketty clackerty
Clackerty BONG
The w__ __ __ __ __ __ __
m__ __ __ __ __ __ __
Has gone terribly wrong.

Jean Kenward

Ask the students to read the poem and fill in the missing words from the chorus.
Read the chorus again, with the teacher reading the first part of each line and the students making the sounds.
Explain that the word comes from the Greek *onoma* = 'name' and *poiein* = 'make'.

Onomatopoeia

You can use onomatopoeia in your descriptions. For example:
dead leaves "crackle, crunch and have a crispy sound"
kangaroos jumping "ca-thumpa, ca-thumpa"
drinking through a straw "slurp, suck, splash, sip".

3 Write sound words in the phrases.

Keerack

a The ____________ and the ____________ of the thunder in the sky

b The ____________ and the ____________ of some coins in your pocket

c The ____________ and the ____________ of the birds in the trees

d The ____________ and the ____________ of the wolf as he blew the house down

e The ____________ and ____________ of your heart after the race

4 Write sound verbs which best match the words.

a a car horn ____________

b the sound of a small bell ____________

c a police siren ____________

d water from a tap ____________

e sprinkling rain ____________

f a chopping axe ____________

5 Write sentences which include at least two sound words for each word below. (The first is done for you.)

SPLAT

a thunder The storm clouds came together and then there was a mighty rumble and boom of thunder.

b cats ____________

____

c bees ____________

____

d kettle ____________

____

Tick Tock

6 Choose words to describe the sounds.

quiet talk ____________ the sound of rain ____________

Your turn to write

Grrr!

Become a word collector. Collect words which:

- sound good, like *giggle, hiss, billabong*
- sound-like noises, like *buzz, sizzle, chirrup*
- are interesting place names, like *Boomoonoomoonah, Nar Nar Goon, Skull Creek*
- are made up, like *chortle* (taken from 'chuckle' and 'snort'), *chuckle, burble.*

Collect them, write them, say them, memorise them.

Antonyms

Antonyms are words with opposite meanings.

That's Good, That's Bad

Read this story with a friend.

A man went for a trip in a plane.
—Oh, that's good!
No, it's bad—the plane had a faulty motor.
—Oh, that's bad!
No, it's good—he had a parachute.
—Oh, that's good!
No, it's bad—the parachute collapsed.
—Oh, that's bad!
No, it's good—he landed in a haystack!
—That's good.
No, it's bad—there was a pitchfork in the haystack.

Antonyms

Antonyms are words with opposite meanings. For example, the opposite of 'good' is 'bad'.

Read the poem and do the activities.

1 Write antonyms for these words.

good ________	up ________	over ________	happy ________
huge ________	he ________	hated ________	bottom ________
ugly ________	best ________	nothing ________	give ________
weak ________	wet ________	below ________	stop ________

2 Choose an antonym for each word and write it in a sentence.

a begins ________________________

b west ________________________

3 Write an antonym to fit the squares for each word.

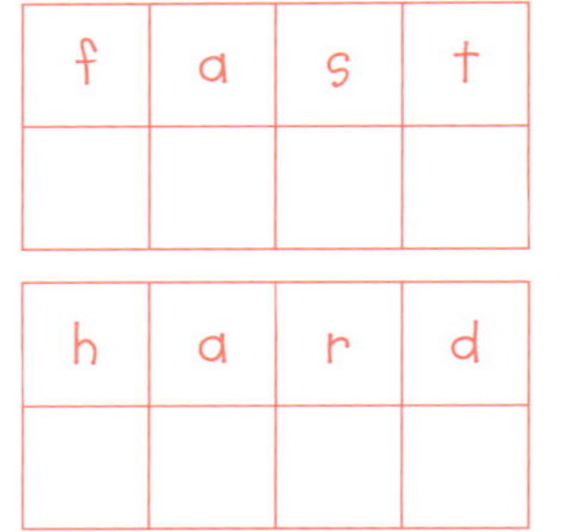

w	e	t

f	i	r	m

a	b	o	v	e

n	e	w

l	o	v	e

b	l	u	n	t

Play a game of 'Opposites' with the students. When the teacher gives an instruction, everyone must do the exact opposite. For example, "Close your mouth, open your eyes and don't talk to your neighbour."

Unit 29

Prefixes

A prefix is a word part which is added to the beginning of a word. It changes the meaning of the word. For example, *un* + *fair* = *unfair* (the opposite of *fair*).

4 Add the prefixes *un-*, *in-*, *dis-*, *mis-* to make antonyms.

a ______________fair **b** ______________correct **c** ______________spell

d ______________appear **e** ______________zip **f** ______________selfish

g ______________plug **h** ______________take **i** ______________believe

5 Write in the missing words, using prefixes. The antonym is in the brackets.

a Hitting him was an ________________________ thing to do. (kind)

b I ________________________ eating Brussel sprouts. (like)

c If you ________________________, you get into trouble. (behave)

d When you are ________________________, you should not come to school. (well)

6 Create the antonyms by adding 'n't'.

would + n't = wouldn't must + n't = ______________

does + n't = ______________ have + n't = ______________

Beware! When you add 'n't' to a word like 'will', the whole word changes: 'won't'.

7 Use the antonyms to solve the puzzle. When you have completed it, read down the higlighted column to find what bad thing was in the haystack.

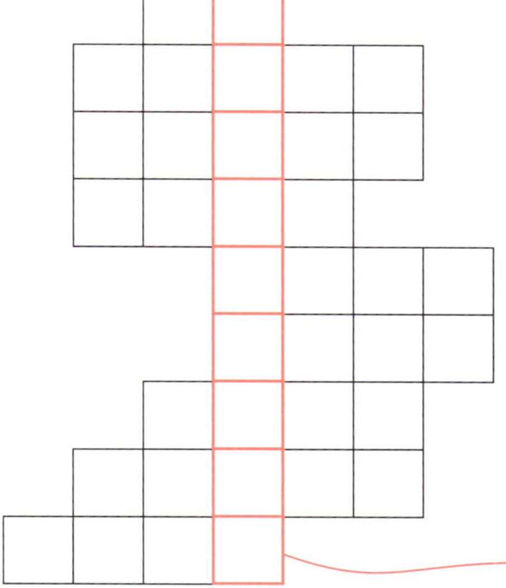

a down
b bald
c before
d poor
e easy
f empty
g bad
h better
i well

The bad thing at the bottom of the haystack was a

___ ___ ___ ___ ___ ___ ___ ___ ___.

Make a class 'That's good, that's bad' book. Work with a partner. Each pair produces one page of the 'That's good, that's bad' book, based on the model opposite. Choose a starting line. It could be:

- A man went for a swim
- I went to the dentist
- A spider crept into the tent at night
- Two boys stayed away from school
- It was Dad's birthday
- The teacher was away.

Synonyms
A synonym is a word similar in meaning to another word.

Synonyms for the word like are admire, fancy, be fond of, be keen on.

Remember: Antonyms are words opposite in meaning to other words. Antonyms for like are dislike, hate.

Inspirations

Invitation!!

Care for our environment at school!

Become an ***inspiration***.

Who is invited? Anyone at school.

What is required? Write a letter saying why you would make a good inspiration member.

When? Closing date 8 March

Who? Write to me—Mrs Kerr, Grade 4K at school

Write now! Don't miss out!
Join the Inspirations Team.

2 March

Dear Mrs Kerr

I would like to become an inspiration because I love nature and helping the environment and that is what being an inspiration is all about!

I would love to save the big animals such as tigers, elephants, the pandas, whales and heaps more endangered wildlife animals.

I also want to stop pollution from continuing. If I am chosen to be an inspiration, I would love to help out with rubbish-free lunches and WILL go to every meeting unless I am away.

I would love to be involved with the inspirations, so please pick me.

From Jessica P, Grade 4a

Synonyms Many words have similar meanings. When you are writing, try to choose the best word, not just the first one that comes to your mind.

Read the transactions and do the activities.

1 Choose the most suitable synonym for each gap.

a (like / love) I would ____________ to become an Inspiration, because I ____________ nature.

b (jot / write) When you ____________ a poem, it's a good idea to ____________ down some notes first, before you ____________ down a final draft.

c (note / letter) I'll write a quick ____________, because I don't have time for a ____________ .

d (finish / stop) Please ____________ the sentence and then ____________ writing.

The transaction shows an interaction between two people—a student and her teacher. The transaction involved the posting of an invitation on the school notice board and a letter of application by a student. Note that the letter is less formal, but includes the date, opening greeting, information randomly grouped and a signing off.

Synonyms for overused words

Synonyms for the word *big* in the *Australian Primary Thesaurus* (Oxford University Press)

fat	giant	huge	bulky
great	colossal	enormous	gigantic
jumbo	hefty	large	immense
lofty	tall	king-sized	mammoth
massive	mighty	monstrous	monumental
outsize	spacious	stupendous	
	tremendous	vast	

How can I find a synonym for the word "big"?

Look up a thesaurus.

2 **Some words, such as 'big', are overused in students' writing. You can often choose a better word by using a thesaurus. List as many synonyms as you can in each box, then use a thesaurus to add to your lists.**

said	nice	good

3 **The synonyms for this puzzle are from the letter or invitation.**

Across
1 finish
3 love
4 excellent
5 assist
6 beasts
7 lots
8 garbage
9 protect (look after)
10 absent
11 jot down
12 selected
13 midday meal

Down
1 rescue
2 choose
3 note
9 finishing (date)
14 wish for

Your turn to write

Think of a big issue at school which is of particular interest to your class (litter, pet care, a charity, healthy food). Work out how your group or class can make a difference. Plan how you will go about and then design an invitation to post on the noticeboard, asking others to join in.

Self-assessment

Recount – A recount retells a series of events in the order that they happened.

	Yes	No
Purpose: Does it tell about past events?	☐	☐
Structure: When I write a recount, I include:		
• an orientation telling who, where, when	☐	☐
• a series of events in order	☐	☐
• a personal comment.	☐	☐
Forms: I can write:		
• a diary extract	☐	☐
• a personal letter	☐	☐
• a postcard	☐	☐
• an email.	☐	☐

	Yes	No
Grammar: I have used:		
• common nouns, e.g. shop, tin, school	☐	☐
• proper nouns, e.g. Tom, Sydney	☐	☐
• personal pronouns, e.g. she, him, we	☐	☐
• past-tense action verbs, e.g. jumped, walked	☐	☐
• time and sequence words, e.g. first, next	☐	☐
• adverbial phrases, e.g. with a hammer, in the car.	☐	☐
TOTAL	☐	☐

Information report – An information report gives accurate and factual information about a class of living and non-living things.

	Yes	No
Purpose: Does it give information about a class of living or non-living things?	☐	☐
Structure: When I write an information report, I include:		
• general statement	☐	☐
• series of facts.	☐	☐
Forms: I can write:		
• a science report	☐	☐
• an information chart.	☐	☐

	Yes	No
Grammar: I have used:		
• common nouns	☐	☐
• technical nouns, e.g. mammal, oxygen	☐	☐
• present-tense verbs, e.g. swims, grows	☐	☐
• quantity adjectives, e.g. few, some, many	☐	☐
• classifying adjectives, e.g. **tropical** fish	☐	☐
• adverbs to describe action, e.g. fly **rapidly**	☐	☐
TOTAL	☐	☐

Procedure – A procedure gives instructions on how to make or do something.

	Yes	No
Purpose: Does it tell the reader how to make or do something?	☐	☐
Structure: When I write a procedure, I include:		
• goal	☐	☐
• materials	☐	☐
• steps.	☐	☐
Forms: I can write:		
• a recipe	☐	☐
• instructions on how to make or do something	☐	☐
• the rules for a game	☐	☐
• directions.	☐	☐

	Yes	No
Grammar: I have used:		
• present-tense action verbs e.g. climb	☐	☐
• adverbs e.g. carefully	☐	☐
• commands, e.g. Count the number of heartbeats.	☐	☐
• conjunctions, e.g. and, but, or	☐	☐
• time and sequence words, e.g. before	☐	☐
• factual adjectives about size, shape, colour.	☐	☐
TOTAL	☐	☐

Self-assessment

Exposition – An exposition consists of arguments from one or more points of view.

	Yes	No
Purpose: Does your text argue or persuade from one or more points of view?	☐	☐
Structure: When I write a persuasive text I include:		
• statement of position (my point of view)	☐	☐
• arguments for and/or against my point/ points of view	☐	☐
• concluding statement (restatement of my point of view).	☐	☐
Forms: I can write:		
• an argument	☐	☐
• a discussion	☐	☐
• a persuasive poster.	☐	☐

	Yes	No
Grammar: I have used:		
• common nouns, e.g. adults, rubbish	☐	☐
• pronouns – personal and possessive	☐	☐
• present-tense verbs	☐	☐
• sensing verbs (to describe feelings), e.g. think, enjoy, wish	☐	☐
• relating verbs, e.g. am, is, can	☐	☐
• time words to link arguments, e.g. then, after.	☐	☐
TOTAL	☐	☐

Explanations – Explanations explain how and why things happen or how something works or has formed.

	Yes	No
Purpose: Does it explain how or why something has happened?	☐	☐
Structure: When I write an explanation, I include:		
• identifying statement	☐	☐
• explanation sequence	☐	☐
• summary statement.	☐	☐
Forms: I can write:		
• an explanation produced as a result of a question and research-based answers	☐	☐
• a flow chart or explanatory diagram	☐	☐

	Yes	No
Grammar: I have used:		
• technical nouns, e.g. earthquakes	☐	☐
• action verbs e.g. vibrates, flows	☐	☐
• present tense e.g. crashing	☐	☐
• adverbial phrases telling how, when, where	☐	☐
• text connectives that show cause and effect, e.g. because, if, when	☐	☐
TOTAL	☐	☐

Narrative – A narrative tells a story or entertains readers by telling a series of events with a problem and a solution.

	Yes	No
Purpose: Does it tell a story or entertain?	☐	☐
Structure: When I write a narrative, I include:		
• an orientation telling who what where	☐	☐
• a complication, a problem	☐	☐
• resolution: the problem is solved.	☐	☐
Forms: I can write:		
• a story or play	☐	☐
• a myth, fable or legend.	☐	☐

	Yes	No
Grammar: I have used:		
• common and proper nouns	☐	☐
• personal and possessive pronouns	☐	☐
• adjectives	☐	☐
• past-tense verbs	☐	☐
• conjunctions	☐	☐
• time and sequence words	☐	☐
TOTAL	☐	☐

Self–assessment and reflection:

Cross-Reference Chart

Key
Unit number–**Page number**

Focus	Book 1	Book 2	Book 3	Book 4	Book 5	Book 6
Nouns – common	1–6, 2–8	1–6, 2–8	1–6	1–6	1–6, 4–12	1–6
Nouns – proper	4–12, 5–14	4–12, 5–14	2–8	2–8	2–8	2–8
Nouns – collective				4–12	3–10	4–12
Nouns – technical						3–10
Nouns – plurals	6–16	6–16	3–10, 13–30	3–10	6–16	5–14
Pronouns	10–24	10–24	14–32	5–14, 6–16	5–14	6–16
Adjectives	8–20, 9–22	8–20, 9–22	4–12, 5–14	7–18, 8–20	8–20, 9–22	8–20, 9–22
Verbs	11–26	11–26, 12–28	8–20, 9–22, 10–24	10–24, 11–26, 12–28	10–24, 11–26	10–24
Verb tense	12–28, 13–30				12–28	12–28
Adverbs	15–34	15–34	12–28	13–30, 14–32	15–34	13–30
Prepositions	16–36	16–36	16–36	23–50	16–36	15–34
Phrases		17–38		24–52	17–38	16–36
Conjunctions	22–48	25–54	15–24	22–48	18–40	17–38
Subject and predicate						18–40
Clauses				25–54	13–30	19–42
Simple sentences	17–38	18–40	11–26, 20–44		28–60	20–44
Compound sentences					28–60	20–44
Complex sentences					19–42	20–44
Statement		19–42			21–46, 29–62	23–50
Question	18–40	20–44	18–40	17–38	21–46, 29–62	23–50
Exclamation	19–42	21–46	19–42	18–40	21–46, 29–62	23–50
Command		13–30			29–62	11–26, 23–50
Full stops	3–10	3–10	6–16, 7–18		21–46	
Capital letters	3–10	3–10	6–16, 7–18			
Commas			21–46	16–36	22–48	
Apostrophe – of possession				19–43	23–50	24–52
Apostrophe – of contraction	20–44	28–60	17–38	19–42	24–52	25–54
Direct speech	27–58	27–58	22–48	20–44	25–54	26–56
Indirect speech						26–56
Paragraphs						22–48
Synonyms	23–50	23–50		30–64	27–58	28–60
Antonyms	24–52	24–52		29–62	27–58	28–60
Compound words	26–56	29–62				
Figurative language		30–64	29–62	27–58		29–62, 30–64
Alliteration	29–62	30–64	30–64	26–56		
Onomatopoeia	30–64	30–64		28–60		30–64
Metaphor						30–64
Review units	7–18, 14–32, 21–46, 28–60	7–18, 14–32, 22–48	23–50, 24–52, 25–54, 26–56, 27–58, 29–62	9–15, 15–34, 21–46	7–18, 14–32, 20–44, 26–56, 30–64	7–18, 14–32, 21–46, 27–58